47 PALM STREET

WERK-EN RUST,GEORGETOWN, BRITISH GUIANA, SOUTH AMERICA

CHRISTINE-ALTHEA RUTHY RICHARDS-LEVI

Our home 47 Palm Street.

Picture shows author in 1966 Werk en Rust Georgetown Guyana South America.
Christine Althea.

CONTENTS

MR RABBIT

47 Palm Street, Werk en Rust,
Georgetown, South America.

YummiesPartnershipPublishing©

COPYRIGHT

This book is sold subject to the conditions that it shall not, by way of trade or otherwise, be lent, resold, hired out or otherwise circulated without the author's prior consent in any form of binding or cover other than that in which it is published and without a similar condition including this condition being imposed on the subsequent purchaser.

Disclaimer:

This book is a fictional dramatisation based on the true story, real events and was drawn from a variety of sources including interviews and published materials. For dramatic and narrative purposes, the book contains fictionalised scenes, composite and representative characters and dialogue and time compression. It reflects the author's family present recollections of experience over time. Some names and characteristics have been changed and some events have been compressed along with dialogue which has been recreated.

A copy of this book is available at the British Library

Hardback ISBN 978-19996464-0-0
Paperback ISBN 978-19996464-4-8
E book ISBN978-1-9996464-6-2

Yummies Partnership Publishing Inc. ©

DEDICATION

Dedication :

Thank you to Jesus Christ our Lord and Saviour.
To My Great,
Grandfather George Brown and Great Grandmother "Queenie"
Evangeline Brown , Granny Beatrice Eudora Richards nee Brown,
Grandad John Augustus Richards and my Mother Lynette Evangeline
Richards-Lorde. SRN. SRM .
Thank you for all Your Love, Diligence, Industriousness, Inspiration
and Courage. xxx
Chrissy :)

FOREWORD

Thank you for choosing to read our family's story in this unique book. The story is based on true facts as told and handed down from our ancestors and historical geographical facts over 150 years and 5 generations how their families and our ancestors and all that they experienced.

It is a journey to find a true home.

The phrase "Home is where the heart is." rings true throughout each phase and growing closer and ever closer to the final place where all ambition will be fulfilled. The lives my colourful ancestors and family enjoyed love, friendship, misfortune heartbreak and humour.

Jacob Levi a Russian Immigrant was running away to Jerusalem and the promised land, a better life, safety and security. Jacob would escape the pogroms the cruelty death and depravation of life in The Pale Settlement Region and his family would struggle to survive through colonialism, slavery and ultimately Marxism and work hard to achieve their dreams of a better future for this family.

Read along to see if they achieve his dreams and whether they established themselves and found happiness and most important a place to call home. Faithfulness in God intertwines within the story and Love stitches the story together. Escape with Jacob from the bitter cold winters of the Northern hemisphere Russia, Prussia and England to the equatorial sunshine and warmth of South America and ultimately to emigrating to Israel and returning to Christianity.

47 Palm Street is the real home and address of a simple wooden white washed building in the area called Werk en Rust (Dutch name for Work and Rest) in the city of Georgetown in British Guiana now known as Guyana. The street comprised of about 20 different styles of homes gained its name from the statuesque Palm Trees at the end of the street by the watery creek.

British Guiana was a colony of Great Britain until 1966 when independence was granted and the name was changed to Guyana. The land's name was given from the Amerindian language which means Land of Many Rivers. Almost the size of England with a wealth of minerals gold, diamonds bauxite, oil and amazing natural waterfalls like Kaietura Falls

5 times higher than Niagara Falls and the jungles having all manner of flora and fauna. A Small population of just seven hundred thousand citizens in such a vast landmass. Back to our residence a beautiful scene and a friendly street where everyone knows and cares for each other. Number 47 is on the left-hand side as you enter the street. The building is in a symmetrical style composed of simple clapboard style wooden slat planks window panes of various patterns clear ones at the top and frosted ones at the bottom. It is painted white with a sky-blue door adorned with brass numbers 47 made by the youngest son Vincent Richards from an old de fused shell from the British Army. There is a short path with a little wooden bridge over the gully where water flowed and small fish and frogs lived happily coexisting with the family living there. The garden consists of a small strip of iron rich earth where a household kitchen garden with vegetables and fruit grows and a grand cockerel proudly announced the time according to the sun and there are various fruit trees for the folk to enjoy. Enjoy this tale of ordinary folk achieving extraordinary ambitions.

It's a place synonymous with "home" …what is the definition of home

when you traverse continents, countries and civilisations in search of
that special place where at last rest, reciprocity, joy and happiness
security can be found.

The protagonist is our Maternal Great, Grandfather Master Jacob
Levi who is a Jew from Russia who went across land and sea to find
rest and a safe place only hoping that one day his ancestors would be
able to visit Jerusalem. He became George and take on a new belief.

May you be blessed in your going out and coming in.

"Bless this House."

The Guyanese blessing for the home.

Bless this house, Oh Lord we pray.

Make it safe by night and day.

Bless these walls so firm and stout,

keeping want and trouble out.

Bless the roof and chimney tall,

Let thy peace lie overall.

Bless this door that it may prove ever open,

To joy and love.

Bless these windows shining bright

Letting in God's heavenly light.

Bless the hearth a blazing there

With smoke ascending like a prayer.

Bless the people here within,

Keep them pure and free from sin.

Bless us all that we may be fit

O'Lord to dwell with thee.

Written by Helen Taylor and M.H.Morgen aka Brake.

http://youtu.be/fxbr1fXjoy8?

list+OLAK5uy_mTb5fVb0L02PH30RmgdB4Yk9r0S3hPSVQ

MAP OF THE PALE SETTLEMENT
REGION 1761-1917

Map source :Atlas of modern Jewish History by Evyatar Freisel. ©

UMAN, VILLAGE THE PALE SETTLEMENT CIRCA 1881

*H*ow do you know the Jews of Uman from the local Russians?

Easily in the 18th century the Jewish folk who lived in the region of The Pale wore modest clothing, men and women covered their heads men grew long peyotes and had their ever present tszits . Married women wore long sleeved dresses with high collars and they covered their pretty long hair with colourful scarves, young ones kept their hair in 2 fat braids. The Orthodox Christian Russians of the town tolerated them but they were suspicious of their ways hated inwardly and envied them.

The Prayer Tallit's shawls covered their shoulders and strings of tszits swaying with every step .The bearded men of age walked in a permanent haste running to do a mitzvah or to their work and families. They shared the same village but totally separated lives in every aspect language, dress food and belief and much more.

*U*man was at this time period in the area then known as the Pale Settlement first initiated by Catherine The Great in 1791 to contain and restrain the Jewish Population. Jews had been in

Russia for centuries and they could trace back their origins to the 14th Century. Now they had been restricted to this special area of Russia which also incorporated what is now called Prussia and Poland. They were forbidden to live or prosper in their cities such as Kiev and were thus forced to live in shtetels and villages like Uman, which was some 300 km from Kiev.It was a perfect settlement....It looked like a scene from Fiddler on the Roof but without the melodic lilt of the happy tunes. Career paths open to Jews were severely limited restricting social acceleration and mobility only allowing a tiny percentage to attend university.

 n a nutshell the restrictions were as follows:

1. Jews were forbidden to settle anywhere in cities and were forced to live outside the towns, agricultural communities and in designated shtetels naturally this included forced national conscription which could last anywhere from 3 years to a lifetime.
2. Deeds of Sale and leases of real estate in the name of Jews outside of the towns and shtetels were cancelled and repossessed.
3. Jews were forbidden from trading on Sundays and Orthodox Christian holidays.
4. All exemptions given and enacted into law by the lenient emperor Alexander II whose assassination was blamed on the Jews were revoked in their entirety.
5. The new Emperor Alexander III of Russia was determined to crush and bind the Jewish people and forbade almost every positive aspect of life. Finally, in 1892 they became disenfranchised and lost the right to vote.

*J*acob Moshe Levi the original name of our protagonist was born in circa 1868 and by 1881 he had lived his whole life in Uman with his family Mother ,Father and older sister Esther. He and his peers had a hard, poverty-stricken life. Agriculture was their work with seasons and weather dictating every movement and the religious laws their spiritual lives. In Winter the small wooden walled shack they dwelled in with its tin roof and small stove let in the fierce eastern winds and Summer it was just an oven but it was their home and they were justly proud of it. The shul or Synagogue was the most important building in Uman for them and it was also most exquisitely decorated with blue, gold and white paint and held one of the the precious Torah scrolls. Men and women prayed separately divided by a curtain .It was here they prayed daily and it served as educational institution and welfare post for those who had fallen on hard times. Simply it was a sanctity from the dystopian reality of the outside world, here they could dream of Jerusalem and peace on earth. The Great Czar Alexander III ruling from afar, who never visited however he left his footprint on their lives.

The ever-increasingly draconian laws were designed to have maximum negative impact on the lives of the Jewish population in particular, but they would make sport of the serious issues …Joking if the Czar could tax the air he would …as it was they paid over the odds for survival and the existence they endured was pitiful. Hovel homes with no running water and shared facilities with several families….It was hard.

Kept the home kosher. Struggle to survive was from morning till night and they even slept with one eye open as at any time danger could come, always watching the door to see if an unwelcome visitor like the Cossacks was coming to inflict more pain in yet another purge.

The soldiers were conscripted and received bonuses when they were cruel to the Jew. Many thought themselves superior and even noble for their religious beliefs and never forgave the Jews for their perceived blood libel and they blamed them for all their woes. Too much rain Blame the Jews, too much Sun the same ,poor harvest the Jews and so on …It was wretched. Each new birth of a precious child increased their population but sustained and fuelled the hatred and jealousy.

*E*aster was when it was the worst time for danger. With celebrations of the triumph over death with the resurrection of the Christ Saviour being revived. The story of the crucifixion would be whipped up from the pulpits of the Orthodox Christian Church and they relished retelling the story with more gusto each year. The Jews stuck doggedly to their faith never wavering from it.

They refused to convert to Christianity to have an easier life. Heaven Forbid so they were pursued as they faced a choice of converting to Christianity or be dammed to endure never ending scorn. In this atmosphere each Jew could expect a life that was seldom sweet or long only Shabbat was a feast and they would look forward to it as their weekly reprieve. The other villagers would sometimes violate the Jewish Shabbat by working on the Saturday louder and harder than on the other days. The Christians saw it as their mission to convert them and tried their level best..

What to do, this was the life and God willing one day they would be free and able to worship in Israel the promised land and be able to celebrate and live without fear and despair. Parents dreamt that if they didn't make it there then their children would one day be able to really live in peace and they would have a home in Israel the Jewish home land …for this they lived, hoped and prayed. For this they kept the traditions and remained Jews despite all normal contingence stating it was obviously no way to survive. They chose to stay Jews regardless of all they endured.

The future generations would one day find the happiness in the Land of milk and Honey.

The Levi family Father Abram, Abba, Mother Hannah, daughter Esther and son Jacob lived in a two roomed wooden shack in the centre of Uman. It was always clean, neat and tidy and welcoming. On Shabbat a tiny emaciated chicken adorned the Shabbat Table surrounded by vegetables chopped pickled herrings and two home baked plaited Challot loaves. All was lit by two candles and the blessing was spoken by Mother with the candle light illuminating the room with the tranquillity of the holy light erasing the harshness of their reality. Around the Special table they ate heartily and dreamt of happy times and sang hopeful tunes . Avram read the Torah portion for the week and they all listened attentively and enjoyed what was to be their last Shabbat together although they knew that not.

The Rabbi had taken up the habit of praying each morning very early in the caves above the village which he had fashioned into a secret safe alternative shul, a good storage place for the scroll. In the morning after his 13th birthday and his bar mitzvah Jacob was able to join the minion, so while all were still asleep Jacob rose early and joined the Rabbi Jonathan. Jacob had been chosen to make up the minion of 10 men to say the daily prayers for thanking Hashem and entreating God to give well-being to the Jews of Uman and the world.

Yet another decree had come from the Czar :All the Jews in the region were to be taxed double and were to be compelled to join the army for up to 30 years conscription .They would no longer be allowed to leave the country or to travel freely .The Jews protested. Rabbi had taken the decision to make the cave shul had protected the Torah scroll and the other Synagogue implements. The ten men left at four am just before the cockerels announced the new dawn and they had just finished their prayers Thanking God and asking for God's help and support when the thunderous horses and shouts of the Cossacks and local people arose from the village ...the shout went out from the attackers "Everybody out end of our woes Jews out !!!"Smashing glass ,screaming shouting some even singing Orthodox hymns women and children took part in the destruction.

The Pogrom leaders came armed with cutlasses guns, machetes, knives and fire. They surrounded the hovels and kicked in doors smashed windows and killed everyone they found inside regardless of age or gender. Those that tried to flee were captured and thrown into the river to drown or had their heads beaten against the trees. So many Jews were killed that the river ran red with their blood of the souls. After all was done the bodies were piled up in large pits and their humanity looted of their gold and treasures. The women of the village took over the deceased jewish homes stealing the furniture, pots pans and clothing anything of value was looted. The rabbi and his 10 men hid in the safety of the cave until it was felt to be safe.

When nightfall fell only then did the total destruction of the thousands of Jewish souls end and the clear up begin with the total acquisition of their former neighbour's property become a formal fact.

The ten men above in the caves were the sole survivors of the carnage and they said Kaddish for the souls who had been massacred. They came down and wept when they saw the total destruction of the village and synagogue, realised the wisdom of the Rabbi in taking the precious Torah scroll to safety. Quickly apprising the situation Jacob cried like a baby when realised he was now an orphan and had lost everyone and everything. They walked gingerly towards their old homes, sparks of hope seeing then a light with candles in the windows but around their tables were other people strangers …if they dared ask for their relative they were met with drunken humour, scorn, guns and knives. Told "Leave while you can !"

It was the end of yet another purge and the Rabbi instructed them and advised the group to dissipate and gave them each a blessing, travellers prayer and a portion of the welfare fund . They visited the make-shift grave of their loved ones and remembered their words that every journey was travelling towards Jerusalem. They slept in the cave and left after prayers going their separate ways. The Rabbis wise words on parting were "If in order to survive you need to assimilate and remove your outward jewish signs do so. You must survive and thrive, later your descendants will live in the holy land as Jews but you must do whatever it takes to enable them to live. Go in Peace. Remembering Psalm 107, and the story of Job." He quoted a part and added his advice "Some went out on the sea in ships , they were merchants on the mighty waters. They saw the works of the Lord, his wonderful deeds in the deep...have courage those who will go by ship and be brave. Be Jewish inside always even if you cannot show it without just stay alive. Shalom."

At this time many Jews who had relatives abroad in America were leaving the pale settlement's region and from 1881 -1914 more than 2 million Jews left Russia.

It was not always so horrible there had been happier times when the former ruler was Czar Alexander II father of Czar Alexander III. He was a reformer he emancipated the surfs from serfdom and he built major infrastructure installations in the land like railways bridges and housing. In 1864 the enacted Judicial reforms allowed local assemblies and the vote. Czar Alexander II also removed the heavy duties and disabilities weighing on the religious freedom for the minorities.

He was ahead of his time. His untimely assassination and his young son's assenting to the throne influenced Czar Alexander III to become extremely autocratic and he believed that a Jew had killed his father so this was his revenge. He repealed all the positive measures his father had brought in and transformed them into ever more draconian measures.

It was time for Jacob the orphan to leave Uman forever.

VILLAGE SCENE

A typical Village in the Pale Settlement Region.

"WHEREVER I GO, I AM ALWAYS GOING HOME!"

Circa 1881-1903

*A*t first Jacob and his friends tried to walk with a nonchalant and carefree air so as not to be too obvious, this lasted till they reached the edge of the village of Uman then looking forward they shook the dust from their feet. Jacob looked back one last time and said Shema and Kaddish Jewish prayer once more. He prayed that one day either he or his ancestor would return and it would be a welcoming safe place, one day. For now, he resolved he must survive there was no time for revenge or insufferable hate.

The men came to a junction in the road and broke into smaller groups and as Jacob wanted to be as far away from Russia as possible his group decided to go in a Northerly direction towards St Petersburg and gain a passage on a ship and sail far away from this cold and hostile desolate place. He also understood that it was unlikely that he would return to this land so wanted to see all he could. At Kiev the group split again with them staying with the Rabbi's friends with whom he had good contacts and safe rooms.

Jacob realised that he needed to change his lifestyle and remove all the attributes of his Jewishness and assimilate into society. Some of his friends made their way to Prussia others to Poland .Little did they know that in a few short years they would not fare better due to the war WWI that was to come. Jacob alone went towards his freedom.

He ran not daring to look behind him into the forest and finally on emerging from the safety of the trees, reached a small town where he felt safe and he entered a bar. He ordered a vodka and quietly wept in the corner thinking of his family especially his Mother with he long braided hair covered with its blue headscarf and her welcoming kind warm smile, lips ready to praise and utter gentle words, arms generous in embrace and caress and heart open to love.

The spirit came to him of his father Avram Jacob's Abba who was wise beyond his years possible his senior status bestowed upon him at 12 he became the main breadwinner for his mother... his own father being killed by an earlier pogrom. Avram had abandoned his hopes to study medicine at university when it was banned and became a tailor instead he worked tirelessly on his Singer sewing machine turning out all manner of suits and articles of clothing for the villagers. The constant whirring of the wheel of the machine, blessing old clothes and material with new life so that an entire family could wear the same Bar Mitzvah suit or wedding costume. Avram's Singer machine only rested on Shabbat. His feet were ever tapping out the rhythm on the pedal stepping and the dancing thread marrying itself within the fabric. He had been a kind and loving father knowledgeable in torah and humorous too. Jacobs sister was due to be married she was grown up beautiful and already and great cook and housekeeper she looked forward to making a home with the Butcher Shimon but now all that hope was gone. They were all gone... but he was alive and would live for all of them.

Jacob was a man at 13 years of age and an orphan too alone in the word and yet so grateful to God for his life. He covered himself with his thick jacket and found a doorway where he wished himself sweet dreams for the night until God would waken him in the morning. He would work a few years more before he could reach his goal and freedom.

The next morning, he felt he understood the difference between him and the others in his party the nine who would remain in The Pale Settlement region wished to remain Jews in and out. He realised that he was to become a Jew within, as a Jew without he could be murdered spat upon discriminated he took on this new disguise and Jacob had decided that he would become local no matter what he was going to survive. God would be with him regardless. The peyotes side locks would be the first to go. Each step along the way he became a more secular Jew. A cap hid his curls and he tucked in his tszits into his trousers and looked for the first opportunity to have a haircut. At the barbers he himself took the knife and cut the side locks he had been growing since he was 3 years of age. As he looked at them on the table he stroked them remembering how he had curled them for Shabbat and he caressed them speaking silent prayers of thanks . Now he felt the separateness that was apparent the distance, it was as if the hairs knew they would play no further part in Jacob's journey and they were placed in tissue and put in the inside pocket where they would stay until Jacob could say a grateful goodbye properly at sea.

Every village knew about the Uman pogrom and people praised the brave Cossacks for their service...they were on the lookout for strangers. A usual test was the outward appearance but the best one was to offer pork bacon sandwich and to see if it would be eaten ... Jacob was famished and was offered the forbidden meal of bread and ham at the local tavern as a test which he ate almost gagging on it but that acceptance surely saved his life.

He found wok at various positions such as daily help, labourer finally after a couple of years he arrived in the splendour and glamour of the impressive city. He saw people of every hue, nationality and all manner of languages. Jacob had travelled by foot, hitched rides on carts and even stowed away on a train on his journey. He had chosen to travel North away from Odessa which was closer as he feared being recognised and routed by the Government troops. He looks Jewish tall lanky and with a hook nose he could not disguise he was happy to see other people who were different so he blended in totally.

He observed the sea faring vessels in all manner of ships some with huge masts and others with funnels, they conveyed diverse merchandise and commodities from far flung places to Russia to grace the tables ,homes and peoples of the empire. Here in St Petersburg the citizens were much more sophisticated in the manner of garb spoke beautifully and effortlessly in more languages …Here Jacob heard French English Portuguese and many other languages .He could have easily stayed here a while longer and settled but when the opportunity arose that he could go to London as a ship deck hand on the Empress Catherina he grabbed the opportunity. The irony was not lost on him that the Czarina who had imposed the restrictive anti-Jewish laws was her name sake that would rescue and take Jacob to freedom and safety.

Jacob learnt quickly getting over the sea sickness by sheer will. He scrubbed the decks ran errands, was a look out shimmying up the masts, cooked meals made himself useful. He persevered learning this new craft. There came a time when he could no longer see Russia and then he found a quiet time and he withdrew his curly sidelocks from his pocket and after a short prayer tenderly kissed them and gently cast them upon the seas .He watched them as they lay on the water as if saying adieu then the bubbles enveloped them and they disappeared forever. Jacob wiped away a tear and thought of Jonah and the Whale, he was lost in his thoughts.

"Hey Shipmate…what are you doing? Come on Join us !" came the invitation from Hans his colleague. Jacob accepted the invitation and they drank and sang songs enjoyed the night.

*L*ife on the Empress Catherina was fun and busy each day beginning with a roll call of the crew, name rank and duties were assigned respectively to the gang. The course and weather for the day were told to them also .

Decks scrubbed food was cooked coal was hauled and the job of constantly feeding the furnace in 45 degrees heat. Shovelling coal and wood the sweat pouring off you was one of the tougher jobs ,keeping the ravenous belly of the vessel per nautical mile and of course fishing was done along the way. The whole ship sparkled and everyone lived in relative harmony.

Captain Vladimir was an excellent seasoned captain who ran the ship in a strict but fair manner. Short stature with a kindly bearded face always with his pet parrot for company, he took a special shine to Jacob but always called him George….. Jacob had earns his sea legs and he had acquired a taste for vodka and started to enjoy pork sausages as this was the main fare on the boat this kept them going giving energy for the day. It seemed an endless journey as each new port opened Jacobs eyes grew wider he saw the new peoples, gained new experiences he had only dreamed of and places along the way. Ports of call included Tallinn in Estonia, Gdansk in Poland all along the Baltic Sea into North Sea and into the English Channel they traversed 45 days with a few days stops in each destinations a chance to attend to any repairs, unload and reload cargo and get some action in the local ports. Jacob was now hundreds of miles away from all he knew he had learnt in his torah studies and did not forget them here he reminisced now recalling his bar mitzvah and how his father had fashioned a new suit for him out of an old one and had specially made and embroidered a white satin kippa for him to wear…His portion of the Torah was about the Exodus and how God Parted the Red Sea enabling Moses to lead the Jews to peace and freedom…Now he too had his own Exodus to freedom.

At Amsterdam as with the tradition of all ports of call the local whores of the red-light district came out to greet the sailors each able to gesture and exalt their wares without the need for translators. They were comely maidens of all sorts a real assortment of women. The Captain gave them all a sub on their wages and with-it warnings to be careful and to return on time. Although he had no real desire to do so Igor his bunk mate persuaded him that Amsterdam ladies were not to be missed and persuaded him to succumb to the charms of a middle-aged woman who in some ways reminded him of his mother. It cost a few guilders and she took him to one of the harbours alley ways and there in that dead-end street brothel Jacob lost his virginity. He had in some ways come of age.

She was a large buxom specimen with shoulder length black hair gold earrings a friendly face and a top tooth smile gold trimmed necklaces and rings adorned her arms and chest. She wore a red blouse and blue skirt with several white petticoats as was the fashion but had no underwear as that made her work easier. The bed was brass framed mattress covered with pretty sheets and a patchwork quilt. They became intimate in the dim gas light of the room. She undid her blouse her voluptuous bosom was released and he milked and suckled as a new born kid all the while she stroked and caressed his sex starved teenage body and lifted her skirts to reveal her private parts .Taking his hand she gently rubbed it against her allowing her wetness to saturate him till he was totally aroused and then undoing his sailors' buttons uniform swiftly she carefully placed his erect member within her. It was an effortless and well-worn path and the music began her sturdy body writhing the rhythm of the breaths he made ...he came quickly pumping his uniqueness into her . She held him close while he regained his composure and then let him go .He paid her the monies and dressed himself and walked slowly back towards the ship. As he looked back he saw the nameless woman with whom he had shared everything already touting her wares with another punter. Once back in his hammock he vowed never to go to a prostitute again.

The journey carried on with endless night at watch he began to learn of the stars and got to know them well as the youngest of the crew he was chosen to do the job of night watchman. The stars kept him company and made it bearable. Each port had the same attractions just different languages and settings, same prostitutes and merchants descended like vultures. Jacob decided to use his free time differently now and sought out Jewish Communities and re acquainted himself with his faith .It was refreshing for him to see Jews able to live and worship in safety and freedom. It stopped the homesickness .

On finally reaching Portsmouth he was glad to be on shore and he and his shipmates had become firm friends they had a tot of rum and he parted as friends thanking them for all they had taught him. Indeed, in just 6 short weeks he had become an accomplished sailor and got an excellent reference from Captain Vladimir who had been so kind to him. He would easily be able to persuade another merchant ship to take him abroad. But first to see the sights of London, Jacob made his way there and he was in awe of the sites Parliament, the Thames, St Pauls, Tower Bridge, the wide streets of Regent street, the people the fashion an amazing place and he was free.

At his lodgings the other sailors told of the sugar trade ships and the far-off sugar plantations and how good life was in the West Indies and how the girls were as brown as berries and sweet natured and kind. The sun shone and life was free and easy there.

This was a paradise somehow, he had to be there, he worked on improving his English and practised until he was excellent. He worked unloading the ships on the docks Hays Wharf was his base. Jacob was a hard worker the foreman soon noticed his aptitude and decided he was ripe for training … He stayed at the docks for ten years before he was given the opportunity to travel to the West Indies. Slavery still existed although it was being gradually abolished it still was the norm in the region despite slave revolts the cruel system continued.

He left on the HMS Victory Ship that was to sail to Barbados, St Lucia, Jamaica, Grenada and British Guiana. The sugar plantations were owned by Edward Chauncey Luard a Welsh robust man who obviously enjoyed his product. Later the sugar would be sold to the Henry Tate and Abraham Lyle company merged in 1930's and became a massively rich company which did much charity within England and the West Indies. Sugar Cane had changed the dietary habits of a nation and the world. For now, the West Indies could monopolise the supply of the sweet sugary needs of the colonies but the sugar beet plant which could be grown in colder climes would enable the colonies to make their own sugar in the future.

To get the job he had decided to change his name from Jacob

Braun to a new English name, he chose George Brown and so the story starts anew. He was chosen as he had proved to everyone that he was competent diligent honest and a good people manager over the last years he had excelled. His humble kind spirit meant he would get on well with the natives and those who worked under him. After a long interview and he was chosen and the job was his for the taking, He set sail after Foreman Rick had briefed him on the best place in the West Indies to go to.

He was perfect for the job being an orphan and thus unencumbered by the accoutrements of family life. Jacob now George had a new name and different identity and was ready to start a great career in British Guiana .

The preparation for the journey was short he returned to his lodgings and packed up his few belongings in his kit bag and reported at the Ship .

He was a passenger this time. The sea sickness was back and even though he was not part of the crew he still helped out on deck. It took 2 months to arrive and they visited several places along the way, George looked forward to landing.

On board ship was full of cargo Cheese Cloth, Salted fish, horses, cattle, cotton bales, salt beef and pots pans and so much more. This time he could sleep in a ship berth but he proffered the hammock always. It was a great voyage each island welcoming beauties waving form the shore, amazing flora and fauna. British Guiana was a low land below sea level so you could not see it on approach then suddenly the blue water dissipates to muddy brown water of the Demerara River and the lush green banks full of forests and cute white wooden buildings along the sea wall the dyke built by the Dutch. Welcoming faces cheered the arrival of the ship and the Clock tower at Stabroek Market chimed welcome at 8am in the morning ... they moored and docked the ship .Captain Bates was an ordered man but he liked women and rum .At each Island along the way he had a wife/woman and family they never knew each other and he was quite the man. They had arrived safely and George Brown the persona of former Jacob Levi the Jewish boy that had left The Pale

Settlement had arrived in the place he was to call home for the rest of his life.

The Plantation was perfect for such a hardworking energetic young man who had a kind heart. He would be gentle towards the Slaves and the inner sense of what was right and he always had the memories of Passover and the freedom from slavery the Jews had received. Swaying Palm Streets beautiful friendly natives promised wonderful times ahead.

NEW YEAR CARD

Card depicting Poor Russians being welcomed to the new world by
rich relatives in America. Circa 1881
5641 Jewish Year. Shana Tova.

GEORGETOWN CAPITAL CITY OF BRITISH GUIANA CIRCA 1900

*G*eorgetown was named after H.M King George of England would also be known as the garden city it was beautiful and vast. Local people waited on the sea wall dyke cheering and smiling waving the ship in.

George Brown adopted Vlada's name for him and surveyed this new land his new home. Here he could stay and thrive, he wondered about the Rabbi and the others and hoped they too found happiness, he was sure he had. Master Barnes was the overseer of the plantation at the LBI Estate La Bonne Intention Estate he was to take over from.

A fierce angry red-faced rotund man who even at this early hour stank of rum he had a foul temper and was apt to whip everyone at his fancy he always kept the whip by him for such opportunities. The Slaves hated him and he them .Barnes felt the only way to get production was to belittle, whip and be cruel to them. They would not miss him when he travelled in two days on the same boat returning to England …Barnes was leaving because his wife had become ill and needed medical care in England. Barnes could not wait to go he found the place loathsome the heat intolerable, irritating mosquitos only the rum kept him happy.

George was to have intensive training as within 48 hours he had to learn all about the estate, the people and the products they made from the sugar cane.

They rode along on the wooden horse and cart and the children ran alongside laughing and playing .the women demurely glanced at him and the men doffed their hats as the LBI carriage passed by. The splendours of Georgetown flew by arriving after an hour to La Bonne Intention, Beterverwagteng estate and the village of Triumph.

British Guiana land mass was highly valued agricultural and mineral rich land and had passed through various colonial owners taking it from the Amerindian peaceful possession by force. The Dutch and French had it first and now it was British. Both the Dutch and French would go on having their own Guianas in this resource rich northern tip of the South American continent.

Place names reflected the mixed history of ownership as each coloniser baptised places in their own vernacular. Beterverwagteng meaning Great Expectations and La Bonne Intention meant The Good Intentions...The homes were wooden shacks and only the masters house was a brick-built home, they were pretty painted in bright cheerful colours it was home.

The old overseer had ruled the place with an iron hand with a whippings and thrashings being meted out for the smallest infraction, even looking at him in the wrong way was reason to be placed in the stocks. His slaves worked so hard to meet targets that they would sleep in the fields so the job could be done and some got eaten by crocodiles or bitten by snakes. The former slaves feared who would come in Barnes place and were minded to revolt if the same regime continued.

George decided he would be a benevolent leader and started to formulate a plan to work with them and make their lives better, he could not wait to get started.

Directly the Mean Master Barnes and his family left for England George called a meeting of the men folk and requested to know what they did for work and how they spent their time outside work. He wanted the children to go to school and the mothers to work only part time to care for the family and this idea was revolutionary. Work although hard and back breaking physical it was not too difficult it was simply planting, caring ,harvesting and sending for processing . The land was accommodating there were rich nutrients and the water required for the plants was easily available.

George implemented a system of partnership and also one day off a week on Sunday. They built a church St Mary Ye Virgin and he gave them funds to decorate it and one of the men became the preacher. During the week the church was used as a school and the children were taught to read and write, on slates with chalk, the adults too.

After all was established they made a party to welcome the new overseer Mr Brown to LBI Sugar Plantation BV. Their prayers had been answered. Everyone brought food and rum flowed, music was played it was a spectacular welcome.

The women were particularly beautiful and George decided the best way to go for peace between black and whites was to do as King Solomon did by marrying out of his race and religion …only how to choose…remembering the story of Esther and the lottery he decreed there would be a beauty contest and he would marry the winner.

GEORGETOWN 1900

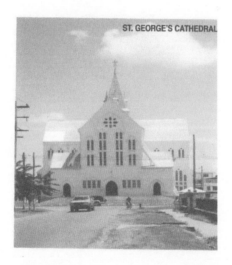

Buildings in Georgetown of note in George Browne's time

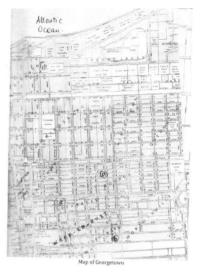

Map of Georgetown

a. Bourda Market
b. 47 Palm Street
c. Stabroek

QUEENIE

circa 1903

*N*otices were posted and announcements were made stating that a beauty contest for all the local girls on the Estate from age 16-26 was to be held at the St Mary ye Virgin Church Church of England church on the 15th April. All were welcome and refreshments would be on offer. The Prize for the winner was to become the legal wife of the new overseer George Brown and thereby freedom as the overseer's wife was a free lady not a worker in the fields.

Of course, word of mouth went around and there was a buzz of excitement, everyone was busy with preparations. Clothes were made ready and patched ,hair braided Sunday best outfits readied, those who had shoes polished them or loaned them, it was to be quite an event.

Two weeks of preparations came to an end at two o'clock in the afternoon. In total there were 140 young ladies all charming and lovely, well most of them.

Daisy was one of the first she looked like a contender until she smiled a toothless grin, then it was over for her. Jennifer was next on the shortlist all looked good until someone stood on her dress tearing it and she ended up in a cat fight as if she was in a boxing ring. The others fell off one by one until Georges personal favourite came by, her bright eyes shone, hair in 2 thick braids and was in a threadbare patch worked dress and had no shoes but was clearly sweet natured and kind. Here was his wife .

Evangeline, Eva for short was only 16 had a lovely smile dark ebony skin, wide eyes and was perfect in every way.

A crown of flowers was placed on her head and a gold necklace and gold earrings were given as presents to her and the runners up. She got the gold wedding band and would become Mrs Brown and her children would be free.

Evangeline left the wooden shack she had called home and moved into the Plantation brick house with its highly polished wooden floors, a four-poster brass bed it even had an inside bathroom and running water .Now instead of serving she was to be served. Queenie aka Eva was now to prepare for the wedding the next day. For the rest of her life Evangeline would be called by her title Queenie

The wedding was quite spectacular and had the desired result with the calming of the tensions of the slaves and there was now tranquillity and peace between the races on the plantation. Children followed quickly first was my grandmother Beatrice Eudora born in Triumph a village close by. Father George Brown chose her name reflecting his tremendous joy at establishing himself and his future. He chose to call his baby daughter Beatrice meaning "She who brings Joy" and Eudora from the Greek "Eu" meaning good and "Doran" gift "The good gift". Then came welcomed siblings Pauline, Hilda, Beryl, Josephine and one son baptised Charlie Brown.

Life was wonderful the owners of LBI were thrilled at how George was making profits for them and gave him profit shares which he shared with the workers. There was always enough to eat it was a happy place. Only his wife and children knew of his Jewish past which came to a point when Charlie was born and George insisted on him being circumcised as was his tradition, he was ready to give up everything but not this. He hoped one day his descendants would reach the promised land. Daily he thanked God for sparing him and letting him live out his days in paradise. George told them stories of his travels and told them if anyone asked that they should tell them father was an orphan from Prussia.

He was happy and safe at last in a place name that meant better expectations which is exactly what he had achieved, more than this he had his Queenie. George gave up Judaism and became a Christian and gave his life to Jesus and he and his family believed.

BETERVERWAGTING BV (BETTER EXPECTATIONS)

circa 1904 -1948

*A*fter Slavery was abolished the former slaves were put off the land and had to fend for themselves for the most part many were reluctant to work on the land for their former masters and Indentured labourers from India were brought in even more numbers leading to racial tensions and riots which still happen even today. The Indians who came were brought over were able to keep their names, families, language and traditions of their Hindu belief. This was a strength that the African slaves had lost through being up rooted from their continent now all these years later not one knew where their ancestral family came from and there was no original language to pass on or any African traditions, all were being lost. In the effort to survive and live the Africans accepted their lot and took on the colonial rulers' laws, customs and they embraced the new Christian religion.

George made a carefully analysed and wise decision to already share the profits he gained all his now free men were happy to continue working with him in Partnership.

George became a Freemason and eventually Head of the Freemasons Lodge of Georgetown. He was to become a prominent business man buying up land and investing in property. The family became relatively wealthy, also the community of BV as it was affectionally called was becoming the place to be. George was also friends with the British Governor and would attend tea parties and the like with Evangeline Queenie. The children were well educated and now at last George could relax a little. The prized wireless radio was shared with the villagers by keeping it on and letting the radio frequency be shared out of the windows and locals would pull up a chair to hear the latest news. In these ways he endeared himself to the locals to whom he was a hero.

On one such evening a cold shudder went through the village it was 1914 and Britain declared that they were at war with Prussia now called Germany… George immediately thought of his fellow Jewish friends who he had left behind in Russia and who had decided to go to relative safety of Lodz and Berlin what was to become of them.?

He prayed as never before, they all did. Indeed, when the British asked for volunteers 70 young men from the village left to fight on the front only 3 returned telling the tales of the tragedy of war and how they had to walk through the fields of Flanders .They brought souvenirs of the war including medals from a grateful nation. Three brothers the Walkers left Georgetown also volunteering only 1 returned, so many left and never returned may they never be forgotten.

After the war the Pale Settlement region was removed and finally there was freedom of movement and the dreadful laws that restricted Jewish life removed. It was replaced with USSR Communism.

Things continued onward progress was being made better infrastructure electricity ,drainage, potable water on tap, hospitals, schools and all the attributes of an improving 20th Century society .Economically things improved with excellent factories creating products for the use in the country ,mining of gold, aluminium, bauxite as well as the food production and of course the sugar plantations. So brilliant was the sugar that the name Demerara Sugar became synonymous with Guiana. These were the golden years.

In 1939 George was enjoying his well-earned success he had become a grandfather already with his daughter Beatrice giving him 2 granddaughters Nancy born in 1928 and Lynette in 1938. Again, he listened to the news from Europe also now they could watch the news at the new cinemas which showed Pathe Films with the latest news from London showing that Britain was again at war with Germany. Again, the British citizens the British Guianese bravely decided to go and volunteer they joined the RAF and infantry and were essential to make the greatest contribution to the war effort but the soldiers suffered from the cold and racial discrimination when the Americans came to England. Even the journey to Great Britain involved acclimatisation as they did not sail directly but via the North Passage close to the Arctic Circle and this was not only cold but an area where the Nazi's were targeting ships with the dreaded U boat. This was the war which some six million Jews would be killed. George knew his friends and family were no more and wept when he heard and saw how Jews were rejected and despised not afforded safety or security he contributed money to assist the war effort and did what he could from afar. Winston Churchill had proposed an ingenious plan in 1939 to enable 250000 Jews live out the war in safety by sending them to British Guiana but Neville Chamberlain the British Prime Minister vetoed this masterful idea thus their fate in Europe was destined for the gas chambers. Eventually Mr Churchill managed to enable some Spanish Jewish refugees to escape, just 50 were allowed to come to Georgetown and they stayed in safety until the end of the war when they emigrated to other parts of South America and Israel.

There was no Jewish Community or synagogue in British Guiana despite of a Jewish presence being there since 1681 when the Dutch Sephardic and Ashkenazi Jews arrived first. After a series of attacks and fires to their properties they all left to make a secure community in Paramaribo in the country next door which was then called Dutch Guiana now Suriname and this still exists today. John would make a pilgrimage to this special Synagogue with its sand floor just twice in his life once for Passover and once for Yom Kippur and the welcome he got there sustained him, only now and again did he have union with a fellow travelling Jew but he prayed privately daily never the less but publicly he would sometimes attend church to be sociable with the community.

Little did he know that in the future the only woman president of Guyana Janet Jagan nee Rosenburg an ardent socialist whose family some say were hanged for treason against USA for spying and collaborating with Russia in USA would be a non-practising secular Jew.

In his old age he succumbed to prostrate cancer and became quiet and prayerful he yearned for Russia and recalled all the memories of childhood. The war finished and the pure horror of the enormity of the death and injuries endured but also that horror of the holocaust was brought to Beterverwagteng a peaceful place. By now George Brown was a good age, he had lived to see in 1948 the forming of the State of Israel . He celebrated and gathering his family together proclaimed the blessing of the Shema and proclaimed "Next Year Jerusalem!" George had been well aware of the world's incredulity, shame and despair when the Holocaust had been made known to the world and then the Balfour Declaration was enacted but first Madagascar and British Guiana had been offered. He found that so amusing but was delighted that Palestine was now too again become his not only spiritual but could become a real place to call home and shout out 'Hear O'Israel the Lord is One...Blessed be the righteous Judge .

May his memory be a blessing" in true safety and shalom.

George was passing on and said to his children as they gathered around his bed that one day they could go to the Promised land and live there. He died and happy and content man finally seeing the homeland and safe place for his people . George was buried on the same day and his tallit was draped over him .His son Charlie read the Shema in English and said Kaddish for him. He would be sorely missed by Evangeline and the children and grandchildren.

George Brown had a street and a corner plot named after him and everyone from the La Bonne Intention Estate mourned and honoured the great man. He had a grand funeral from the Freemasons Lodge and his son in law John Augustus Richards Beatrice's husband gave the eulogy and carried him to his resting place along with Charlie and his entourage was vast. He had chosen John JR out as an upstanding man for his daughter Beatrice as she had divorced the father of her first child Nancy and he wanted her to be settled. John and he got on brilliantly and the marriage to Beatrice was set in the stars and destined for success .George died knowing the future was safe and secure and that his legacy would live on through his legal children Beatrice, Pauline, Hilda and Charlie these were the legal descendants of John and his wife Queenie. It is possible there were children who are also his offspring but these are the legitimate ones.

George Brown the former Jacob Levi had made the right choice as a13 year old young man way back in the days of 1881 in Uman and we thank him for that vision and courage.

JOHN AUGUSTUS RICHARDS AND BEATRICE EUDORA RICHARDS

JR AND DORA.
1930's-1950's

*A*mbition and determination pulsed through the veins of John Augustus Richards. He had been born a twin however on the day of arrival which was unknown and undocumented so he chose April 15th 1900 only he was to emerge alive after the difficult birth and his twin brother's stillbirth. This was the first of many fights he would win in his life. He had a strong belief in his destiny and survival. He was the fittest and could fight the good fight. There was a sense of preordained success within him and he lived for his lost twin all his life. JR was extremely handsome ,intelligent ,tall and elegant strong man. Grey before his year's vanity drew him to always shave his hair off his head of any outward sign of age. This he did every morning ,shining his bald head with castor oil as protection form the equatorial Sun. Beatrice was his second wife and he had 2 sons from his first marriage Buddy the pharmacist and Patrick the filmmaker both lived with their mother whom he supported financially.

Beatrice and JR lived in house he had bought and paid for. It was perched on stilts and had 3 rooms above 2 bedrooms and living room kitchen with and outside privy and inside shower room. Cute and sweet .He had bought the lot number 47 in a street which would be named Palm Street . It was in a new part of town to be called Werk-en-Rust (work and rest) and close to the market of Bourda .

Palm Street was a two-block street topped by Princess Street and Durban Street with Norton street crossing through. At the end of the street was the Le Penenitir Cemetery

(The Repented Cemetery)expanse at the end of the street and gave rest to the locals even though it was prone to flooding. Palm Street was only a short distance from Bourda Market. A great location .

From the top of the street you could look North and see the Vreed and Hoop Terminal (Peace and Hope Terminal)harbour of Georgetown and see the ships docking and the whole city flat and expansive laid out before you. It was to become and inimitable exceptional street typical middle-class neighbourhood with owner occupiers and well cared for homes and gardens. Everyone had a kitchen garden and a pig or chickens and the people loved each other despite the various characters who lived there.

They had made it to live in the city an hour away from Beterverwagteng in the countryside. Beatrice loved her home 47 Palm Street Werk en Rust Georgetown capital city .She had made it and she made every soft furnishing within curtains bedspreads and cushions ,her trusty Singer Sewing Machine working diligently making clothes and furnishing for the locals and British establishment everyone wanted her creations even the governor's wife. The place was just a 5-minute bike ride from the market at Bourda or 15 minutes to Stabroek Big Market by the docks this place was the place to buy anything and everything from household goods, clothes, meat ,fresh fish, furniture such as Berbice chairs chocolate imported Dutch cheese and machinery the other main store was called Guiana General Stores and here is where everything chic could be purchased which was imported from Europe and America. Georgetown was the place to be seen. The huge clock chimed the time and the red roof corrugated roof of Stabroek Market was a landmark to the town .Amerindians would come from the interior of the country taking a couple of days to arrive in the big city. British Guiana was by now a nation of 6 nationalities comprising of Amerindian, Chinese, African , Indian , Portuguese and European white.

The British population ruled the country as it was their colony and there was a Governor General in charge of the country and a judicial system based on British law. The country was a safe secure place but there were rumblings for independence and social reform .

Since WWII the Americans had a base in Guiana and they used to buy the bauxite to make their aeroplanes .they added to the jollity of the country and the economy. Beatrice's skill as a seamstress were in high demand, she had the ability to know instinctively how to cut fabric and could make from sight or picture any garment . JR was working his way up the ladder in the British Guiana Defence Force and then later British Guiana Mayor and Georgetown Council Constabulary Department and soon was promoted he was well known in the area as the local policeman and had endured a couple of attempts on his life from gang land gangsters and petty criminals... but he always won because he knew how to fight even though they used knives and other weapons. JR learnt karate and knew how to use his truncheon. He had been promoted from ordinary police constable to head of the new Bourda Market a large 2 story building with a small clock tower and blue corrugated tin roof basically a slightly smaller version of Big Market.

Bourda Market was named after the Dutch Colonial Joseph Bourda form the 1880's he was the proprietor of the Vlissingen Plantation and he now rests in peace at the Bourda Cemetery. An area of land stretching from Robb Street on the south to Regent Street . John Richards was the tenth Clerk of markets the first in this prestigious role was the Dutch Man Schulder Griffiths who then was in charge of a market that was 12500 square feet by JR's time it was 3 times the size. In the 1940's and 1950's there was growing unrest with the colonial system and it became a space used for political hustings and many prominent politicians spoke and rallied there like Cheddi

Jagan, Forbes Burnham and Walter Rodney who would later be assassinated in 1980 for his political radical Pan African views some say by PNC who saw him as a potential rival for leadership.

*N*ow he was in charge of all he surveyed form his office high in the centre of the market was a great vantage point .His title Clerk in Charge Director of the Market ,he had a trusted group of police constables who ensured order in the market and collected rents. On his highly polished large desk were 2 telephones, behind him was a filing cabinet and he had a secretary and many staff who reported to him. A chart on the wall showed the latest statistics and news of the day and a shipping log noted buyers .There was at this time portrait of King George VI and a map of Guiana. On the desk was a family portrait of Beatrice and the children.

Guiana was still a colony of Great Britain the Mother Country and he was immensely proud to be a citizen of the British Empire. JR was the short version of his long name John Augustus Richards, he was a legend .His middle name Augustus was not given for his birth month which was April on the contrary for the heroic Roman Emperor Augustus Caesar who bore that name and reputation. His parents had great ambitions for their sole surviving twin son. Born into abject poverty and slavery in St Johns parish just 200m from the sea shore of Barbados his parents had made over a few months a make shift sea worthy vessel and somehow attached themselves to it with their child and another family and in the dead of night they escaped the plantation and using the stars and the full moon the traversed the course to freedom.

The owner of the Slaves Master Kimberly had won the family in a heavy drinking and gambling card game from the former owner who obligated to pay or face foreclosure on his mortgaged land. The old callous master was up for selling the offspring of the slaves just as one would sell cattle and JR's parents were determined to keep their little family intact . Mr Kimberly was an free whipping mean fisted man .He worked his slaves relentlessly in the searing heat until they were fit to drop ,the tropical rains flooded out the tiny chattel houses which they had to dismantle and move to wherever the master wanted them to work .The worst was not the constant degradation and meanness but the sheer lack of prospects for education for the children, there was no hope and they heard that in Guiana a black slave man could be free and become somebody and they wanted John to have that chance.

Mary and Joseph were extraordinarily ambitious striving to provide new opportunities for their children. They could read a bit and understood the notices stating that Slave would be sold in a fortnight separating families. His parents knew they had to leave. After a challenging journey lasting some 14 days they arrived in British Guiana .There was nowhere where they could escape the British Empire but some places were better than others and British Guiana was one. They were able to sneak ashore and blend into the community it was a severe crossing but they had survived. The coastal village the landed on was called Paradise they were to work on Rice farms and sugar plantations. Fortunately, they were befriended by the local rice workers and taken to the master who happened to be Mr Richards he gave them his last name and they were then safe...

He made them free men as he saw them not as runaway slaves but free ...a most enlightened man. They were given a home and work. Home was a one room chattel hut on the edge of the plantation Joseph JR's father was an accomplished blacksmith and Mary the mother was a great cook so they found work straight away.

The new plantation gave the children education while the parents worked. Mr Richards was benevolent and instilled discipline and insisted everyone could read and write and encourage further learning and crafts. On the night they left there were hugs and tears all round with the other slaves Joseph and Mary gave a sermon of life trying to put as much wisdom into their children, they had also taught their children to swim. They had dressed warmly and somehow saved some money from odd jobs John had a younger sister who travelled also Josephine .The food they saved all went on the vessel and they put all their meagre possessions on the raft Joseph pushed it out to sea until the water was waist high then he climbed on the experienced fishermen Anton guided them by the stars and they were on their way to freedom.

Along the way in the ship they recalled that they stopped in Haiti and were terrified by the poverty and desolation they saw zombies and the voodoo religion ,they could not wait to leave. Trinidad and Tobago were beautiful islands where some men got off to seek their wives and family who had been sold off the island of Barbados to work there ...they all wished him well and they bought fresh supplies, it was to be a few more days travel.

After John finished his high school education at which he excelled he decided to make his fortune and new money is needed for that so determined to go where the gold was and is .Although he had ability he had no money to attend higher education so had to think outside the box.

JR was to spend almost a year in Venezuela here he found gold and made his fortune .It was not an easy start but his amiable nature and willing ways meant everyone was happy to help and guide him.

It was here JR learnt from the Amerindians to sleep in a hammock, something he would do the rest of his life. His first night in the jungle he cleared a space to sleep on the jungle floor. All manner of creepy crawlies and dangerous animals like jaguars walked there .They taught him which flora and fauna he could eat and use for medicinal purposed, they found it hilarious when the bird call of the Hoopee bird which sounded like a question "Who You?, Who You?" to which John answered " Its me John !" he said this several times until the locals explained it was a bird call and so not to answer it, they wet themselves with laughter .

He saw that no one gets old working in the gold mines so as soon as he had achieved his goal he made his way back to Guiana and Georgetown became resolute to get a career and become a great man of the city he loved with a family to love and cherish .

His values were spot on .

He had come far from his humble beginning he had made it indeed to the top achieving much more than his parents could ever dream. JR was rightly proud of his achievements. John Richards had thanks to his initiative been able to marry Beatrice use the gold to buy a plot of land for a new build home at the vacant lot he had been advised about in Palm Street which he purchased and built a new home for his family in the capital city. He was now an alderman of the city, a top civil servant in the realm and was a member of a most exclusive Freemasons Lodge and wore his uniform apron with tremendous pride. More than all of this he was super proud of his loving family.

By now he had with Beatrice quite a family his 2 children from his previous marriage Buddy and Neville and Beatrice had brought Nancy there had been twin boys but they died in the first week of life then came Lynette, Owen and Vincent lastly a foster child Pansy. It was his wonderful family that gave him most pride and pleasure.

John Augustus Richards and family had achieved, social climbing themselves to become middle class of society in Guyana .

THE FAMILY RICHARDS AT HOME.

© Ruthy Richards-Levi

THE MURPHY FAMILY, MARKET STALL 119,

BOURDA MARKET, BOURDA, WERK-EN-RUST.
1940's

*H*ere we introduce you to some of the characters who operated in the market .Some traders lived hand to mouth making barely enough to eat a meal on a daily basis and sustain their meagre existence. Others managed well and could even save for the inevitable rainy day, like when the Sea Wall broke and the land was flooded flushing all their property away or when the wood ants and termites decided your home was their next meal or sometimes simple a pregnancy, child's school shoes or worst death otherwise illness leading to the Mother or the breadwinner dying would plunge a family into spiralling debt and poverty. Still others made vast profits and lived-in 2 storey villas and had servants .

The Boswell family was one such family in the wealthy class their stalls and shops sold spices, flour, rice ,eggs and other daily staples .They were the biggest traders and renter of stalls in the market. They were extremely polite and friendly to all and were simply kind and honest decent traders and they would have queues of customers waiting to be served. Prices were fair and weigh scales honest always tilted to give an ounce or two more than you paid for but never short. Boswells had property in Palm Street and Princess Street where they also had a printing press business and a beautiful villa. They were loved by all.

The two brothers Boswells were close neighbours in Palm Street, the 2 brothers both staunch bachelors lived together and had a merry time. They were fun and kind but the created their own population explosion by having between them 10 children... after some time in his 60's the elder Boswell decided to settle down marrying and Hyacinth Boswell Lynette's good friend was born.

*A*s JR made his rounds each day everyone greeted his smiles with Good Morning Mr. Richards his constables controlled all the stores checking the weights and measures and cleanliness of the spaces. His stern looks and quiet warning words reserved for the market traders who were not up to his standard...One such place which was a frequent recidivist was that of the Murphy's family.

Fourteen children in the family. Headed by a famine thin man with a gaunt unsmiling demeanour, small boned creature married to a large fattened sow of a woman. They were the baker family of the Murphy's.

Sigismund was a miser and it was a miserable family it was said there was little or no laughter in the iron rod disciplined home they shared which was no bigger than a normal sized 2 room house with hammocks swinging underneath for the older children to sleep in so overcrowded was it .To make ends meet Siggy the father was a baker and the mother ran a haberdashery stall in Bourda Market and hence their paths crossed with Mr John Richards.

The Murphy's stall was in the third row in a corner at the cheaper end of the market. They traded in haberdashery, ribbons, threads, needles and all sundry of sewing articles for making and finishing garments. A small dimly lit canopied stall consisted of wooden table and bench. Many small boxes separated the items and all was measured out with a

Yard stick. On the bench sat Sheila and Lucille the eldest children of the family .They sat and gossiped all day long passing acerbic comments on all who passed by. Both were naggers and vindictive and had been left by their husbands as was the fate of each of the children not one child had a long-lasting relationship. Either the sons were unfaithful or the wife's daughters were vicious lounged. They condescending to everyone the condescended to serve. Miserly Sigismund had been caught out a few times for short changing or short cutting and JR was watching him.

*W*hen a hapless customer purchased a yard of elastic they could return home with it being just short of the yard. While this gave them, some profit it caused many to complain and go elsewhere for their goods. They were the ultimate short-term thinkers, luckily the bread shop was run by the Mother and she was good humoured so that was where the bulk of income came in.

They were indeed an odd couple he emasculated and stick thin she obese at over 200 lbs. He was rumoured never to have smiled as he would say what is there to smile about.

JR showed no mercy to cheats so they were constantly on warning.

Once he forced them to close for a month ,it almost ruined them so they tried to keep in his good books giving Lynette JR's daughter almost cost price when she came by to buy goods for Beatrice her seamstress mother. JR would do spot check patrols and Bourda was without a doubt the smartest market in the town and JR was rightly proud of the place. As he moved through stall holders would rush to tidy the area and kept it clean and sanitary. Everyone in Georgetown knew him by reputation as a highly regarded Gentleman.

It was without a doubt the management style encouraging those under him to learn on the job and to study to achieve the most of their potential. In his term as, Chief Market Officer the market continued to have a warm atmosphere and was relatively free from crime.

Lynette Richards enjoyed the high status awarded to by her father's position and as she wondered around the market became efficient to get the best bargains for her family .

Everyone knew her and always gave her the very best.

JR was proud of all his children but especially Lyn ,he wanted her to succeed even if that meant that she would leave to study abroad. For now, all was good she had gained a place at the prestigious school Tutorial and was studying O'levels and A'Levels GCSE's he was full of pride when he spoke about her to others.

Little did he know that in the future many would leave British Guiana that it would become a sad quiet place deserted by all the youth who would leave to go to America, Britain and Canada the ABC countries. It would become a dystopian reality with letters and airmail correspondence would be anxiously awaited not only for welcome news that their loved one or child was still alive and doing well but for the money the offspring would send ,the valuable hard currency would stave off hunger ,pay medical bills build houses and keep families from the brink. Georgetown was to become a place of quiet sadness and solitude of those that would leave only a tiny percentage would return permanently and many would never see the land again tragically.

John Richards could not envisage such a future for now Great Britain was in control and all was orderly, happy, joyous and community life was grand.

SCENE AT MARKET.

Bourda Market today .

LYNETTE EVANGELINE RICHARDS

October 22nd 1938-

Lynette Evangeline Richards was born at home in the bedroom of 47 Palm Street, Werk-en-Rust , Georgetown, British Guiana. A British Subject by virtue of her birth into the colony of British Guiana. The second pregnancy of the marriage of John and Beatrice was a success both Mother and baby were doing well and this child would survive unlike her little twin brothers who had not made it past the first week of life.

Little Lynette was to become the apple of her father's eye and he was exceptionally grateful and honoured by God to have been given this child to love. Grandad John Brown was delighted that his wife Queenie had been honoured by the middle name being chosen and thrilled to have lived long enough to see another grandchild. He bought her gold bangles and earrings to commemorate her birth.

She was as good as gold and relished being big sister to Owen when he came along a few years later and then Vincent the surprise early Christmas gift arrived some 11 years after Lynette's birth on the 15th December 1948. George Brown got to know and see all his grandchildren and he gave thanks to the God of Jacob for allowing him the privilege of old age. Soon after Vincent arrived he passed on.

Determination and ambition marked the family and John Richards, JR knew and advised them on careers and future prospects. He knew there was a wide world out there and he wanted them to achieve.

Lyn's life at the capital city rolled onwards, she went to her work at the colonies Department Ministry of Health as a junior civil servant. Unemployment was extremely high and jobs were like hens' teeth, so very rare. She had attended evening courses to learn shorthand and could now type 60 words per minute. She was always being praised for her diligence, pleasing manner and accuracy so logically soon she was offered promotion to become the personal assistant to the Secretary for the Minister of Health. The extra income would be welcome as she would use it to help her parents out at home. In addition, she was able to learn about the statistics of low births and deaths from the maternal department and this sparked a lifelong interest in improving pre, ante and post-natal care...Although better than before when having a baby meant danger for both mother and child's survival the statistics showed that there was a disconnect between the mothers in the city, country side and the interior. A great discrepancy and woeful lack of opportunities between the classes. Also, wherever the work was arduous such as in the bauxite excavations of Linden, the gold mines even the sugar cane fields men could become disabled easily and had little or no chance of decent medical treatment so were doomed to be deactivated for the rest for their life, a terrible waste and burden on the family leading some to go to the weed killer solution and drink a gulp, committing suicide... a terrible waste and burden on the family.

It made Lynette determined to make a difference to that health care in the land and she wanted to study further but there was no money for that at this time.

The world economic situation was depressed after WWII warfare the sugar production being in abundance was far too much for the market and the prices was no longer sustainable making production unsustainable...the LBI sugar plantation had partially closed causing unemployment to a number of workers and thus JR as senior head of the family was supporting them as best he could. There was no welfare state and the unemployment rate was high. This was 1957.

As luck would have it senior clerk Miss Elaine Murray a school friend of JR told her that she should look out for a special announcement for an advertisement for training to become a Nurse in Great Britain. She said that the Mother Country was ready to give paid training, all the applicant had to do was apply having O' and A'Levels, good health and excellent references. They would need to pay for their own passage and the training would last 3 years. It was to be announced shortly publicly but Elaine already was aware of the new opportunity, being in a senior position, she also promised that she would give Lyn some interview training and a good reference if she applied.

The daughter of John Augustus Richards was intelligent, ambitions and incredibly beautiful. The only similarities between Nancy and Lynette was their prettiness and the same gap smile but for the rest they were opposite, different hues of skin colour, intellect, fathers, demeanour and stature. Free time was spent differently, Nancy spent her time dancing, partying and making sport. Lynette busied herself with extra classes at the Carnegie Centre of the YMCA cookery and Art Classes at the Edward Barrow centre at all times using her time effectively. Of course, there was time for play and fun but no real love interest although she had scores of admirers she was sort of untouchable boys rightly feared JR. Lynette was also an accomplished pianist without the benefit of a piano in the home, she drew the keyboard on paper with black ink and practiced in this way. Her parents paid for the lessons and were astonished and in awe when she achieved Distinction and Grade 8 Pianoforte.

Presently the recruitment information Elaine had alluded to, she was able to confirm and share. The British Empire colonial office had been requested by the then Conservative government Minister of Health Mr Enoch Powell MP to recruit personnel for the new National Health Service. These individuals were to come from the colonies as there was a serious manpower shortage. The recruitment advertisement was place in all the local newspapers and was also on the Pathe newsreel. Here Mr Enoch Powell MP of Edgebaston invited people form the colonies who were already by virtue of their birth in the colonies British Citizen and had British Passports to come and build the NHS. Qualifications for SRN State registered nurse O and A' Levels, State enrolled Nurses basic reading and writing skills and high school diploma.

They were to be healthy, able to pay the £100 pounds or $480 Guyanese Dollars and to have at least £50 pocket money to ensure they could fend for themselves until the course started. Accommodation, meals and training would be given along with a salary during training...after which they could return to their countries or stay on to continue their training and career. A battery of tests was to be carried out and passed, height, blood, weight, background checks , with no criminal record, good family references, good work references, and the same from the church. Dental checks were also included and for many it was the first time they had been to one. The mistreatment via the rudimentary dentistry were restricted to pulling teeth even if a simple filling with mercury was in order the tooth would be removed. Lynette and many others endured this torture and she had a tooth extracted which was to give her lifelong misfortune regarding her teeth.

Let me introduce Father Derek Goodrich who really deserves a chapter of his own. He was an only child of lovely parents May and Hugh. Mr Goodrich the father of Derek had already fought as a soldier in WWI where he was severely injured and had his leg amputated in the process of the recovery. The artificial limb he was issued was a leaden metal and wood contraption and he walked in pain without complaint for the rest of his life. The death and destruction he witnessed was to make him question the validity of fighting wars and cause him to believe all war was a totally futile waste and compromises should be sought before taking up arms against one's fellow man.

When WWII came in 1939 he was not able to fight on the front line due to his injury but he became a contentious objector preferring instead decided to help his country by working with the Civil Service in North Wales doing crucial work at the office there far away from their London home in 49 Strathyre Avenue, Norbury. Derek was a very smart son with a high IQ and he earned a place at the prestigious University of Cambridge here he gained his BA. Tall handsome with winning personality he studies theology MA at Oxford University and history he was a crucial member of the cricket team. After getting an excellent degree he decided to train for the Anglican Priesthood, church of England. He was asked and chosen for the Parish of Georgetown, British Guiana and after a 3-week voyage by ship disembarked at Georgetown Port and began his missionary life.

One of the first of many families he was adopted by was the Richards and he was a most welcome guest to 47 Palm Street. He gave not only spiritual fellowship, genuine friendship and advice but he also really loved the people of the country. It was him who set up all manner of clubs for the youth to engage in learning new skills, giving then extra-curricular activities, stimulating conversation and awakening their minds. Guyana was lucky as Bishop Trevor Huddleston the Anti-apartheid campaigner famous for his friendship with Nelson Mandela all his life… wanted Father Derek Goodrich to come to Johannesburg and join the good fight. As it was Father Goodrich was hailed welcome by the Parish of Georgetown and in no time, he was the most popular priest in the country as he travelled the length and breadth of the country visiting the remotest parts of the realm.

Derek was seen as a brilliant generous gentleman who was eventually to become the Dean of Georgetown overseeing the monumental task of rebuilding the world tallest wooden building the Georgetown Cathedral, St Georges. He dispensed wisdom and love to all and sundry regardless of race or creed. Even today in his retirement home in the College of St Barnabas in Dormans Village, Lingfield, Surrey each week he is visited by some of his former parishioners from Guyana who have come to GB to live and work. At his 90th birthday party over 100 guests came from all over the globe to celebrate. It was he who advised Lynette to apply to study in Somerset , saying this was the warmest climate in England and it was also the most picturesque. Kindly his parents offered to accommodate Lynette when she would arrive for the 2 weeks before her training was to start as their honoured guest. He would stay in Guyana eventually becoming a citizen and gaining the Golden Arrow Award the highest honour in grateful thanks from the nation.

So, it was that Lyn applied and was accepted at the Maudsley Hospital in Taunton Somerset. Taunton was a white middle class town and they had rarely seen black people but they could not have been more welcoming and kinder. Earlier they had US soldier troops stationed in the town including the boxing star Joe Lewis who had enlisted with the US army during WWII :Brown Bomber" and they knew to be grateful for those who came to assist Britain and they were kind.

However, before all these thing s could come to pass first Lynette would have to bring up the matter at the family dinner table that night ...she knew if she saved hard, did not spend money on clothes and luxuries she could in 8 months have her passage so her parents would not have to contribute. Plus , with the exchange rate she would promise to send money home each month. Oh, England what an opportunity! She must grab it! The saying goes in Guiana; Opportunity is like a China Man with his Pig tail when he cuts it off (to become more Westernised)it never grows back, this was true as the many navvies mainly Chinese who build the railways came directly from China and all came with their traditional top knot pig tail hair styles. Gradually after being exposed to life in the tropics they cut them off and never grew them again.

*R*ing, Ring went the bicycle bell heralding her arrival at home. "Mummy I have news for you ... they are recruiting Trainee Nurses in London England and Miss Elaine said I was perfect for the post! Lynette blurted out excitedly. She could not contain her joy overjoyed at this fortuitous news as she knew well what a change it had made for her own grandfather Jacob Levi aka George Brown and thus all their fortunes. Whether John Richards would be quite so enthusiastic to miss his favourite and only daughter was another matter but together with Mummy they would work it out.

Over a delicious dinner of beef stew and dumplings with callaloo Beatrice broached the subject and after a silence that seemed to last an age John said, " Given the current economic climate I would advise you to become a nurse then specialise in midwifery, you will always have work and it is a blessed profession. We all support you and will do everything we can to get you everything you need to apply and succeed. You save your passage and we will get you all the rest. Huge hugs all round were shared and application process begun. They sat down in the living room and listened to the LPs and sang Bless this House pointing at all the places in the hymn after which the death notices came over the radio at 10pm. The country being small everyone who had died that day or week was mentioned on the radio with appropriate sombre music usually Mahalia Jackson rendition of "In The Upper Room."

Outside the usually jovial crickets and frogs sang mournfully along. Lynette slept soundly dreaming of England.

LYNETTE EVANGELINE RICHARDS

© Lynette Richards-Lorde
Lynette Evangeline Richards age 2, October 1939

Father Derek H Goodrich ©
The Goodrich Family celebrate their 50th wedding anniversary in
Guyana staying 6 months.
Mr Hugh Goodrich and his wife Mrs May Goodrich and their son
Father Derek Goodrich.

HOPE DEFERRED 1958

*A*fter saving up the massive amount of $480 Guyanese dollars the equivalent of £100 British pounds over a whole year Lynette had achieved her goal. Triumphant and excited at this great achievement Lynette could now contemplate and imaging the reality of reaching her dream of becoming a nurse, midwife and finally returning to become Matron of Georgetown hospital. It would start with stepping up the gangplank of one of two cruise ships that carried British Colonial citizens to the Mother Country, they were the Oranjestad and the Willemstad ocean liners. She saw herself stepping daintily up the wooden stairs and promenading along the highly polished oiled wooden decks and meeting new people and seeing the world.

Lynette imagined herself admiring the crew in the lily-white livery, being waited on at the tables and dressing in her new clothes her mother Beatrice had made in the latest fashion as designed by her after scanning the fashion magazines that came from Europe. Beatrice was able to recreate anything just from seeing a picture she could also make her own designs and patterns. Many colonial wives including the governor's wife famous blue and white dress came from Beatrice's atelier the governor's wife wore the same dress for 8 years to every ceremony. Lynette heard calypso music and steel bands form the café radio as she travelled along en route home she imagined sandy beaches, something that Guyana being under sea level she had never seen, and then the sights like London like the Big Ben clocktower, red buses and Buckingham palace.

Pushing her bike along laden with shopping from the market she was absorbing the sights and smells of Georgetown all the way home she imagined these were to be her last weeks in her home town. The mango and gynip trees were laden with fruits, stray dogs and cats ever hopeful for a scrap from a shop, table and a little loving stroke ran alongside her and as she turned into Palm Street the hens and chicks in the yards chirped. You could hear the ringing of bicycle bells a funeral party was singing "In the Upper room " at the Merriman funeral home and in the distance the whoo whoo of the distant steam train chugged along. Listening to all the sounds of the city and imprinting them in her heart.

At home her stomach turned to knots and tears pricked her eyes. My God how beautiful was the small stilted 2-bedroom house, place of her birth only 18 years ago. Here she had lived and shared 1 bedroom between 4. Lynette had elected to sleep on the floor alone to gain some privacy. Home smelt of carbolic soap and lavender wax and oozed warmth and love. The welcoming blue door, the stairs with the special creaking step. As she reached out to open the door her mother opened it with a loving smile and welcome hug.

Since Lynette had said she wanted to go and had been accepted officially offered a place Beatrice had been her biggest supported and any spare cash she had made from Dressmaking she had invested in her daughter's future. She was determined the daughter's ambition would be fulfilled and saw in her a chance and potential that had been thwarted by circumstances of her childhood. Back in Beterverwagteng the good times had come to an end and it was the same now all over the place. The era of king sugar on the world markets and the LBI Estate's role in that was in in decline so further education to become a school teacher could not be financed by George and Queenie so her dreams had been curtailed and exchanged for the British imported Singer sewing machine...but first she had to work in the Rice Fields planting paddy and harvesting it washing clothes in the creek which she had a ring side view when her close friend would lose an arm to a swift crocodile while washing sheets. Beatrice saved the meagre wage and paid for tuition learning the dress making trade and vowed to go to the capital city to live, Beatrice had ambitions for all her children and nothing would hinder them.

*L*ynette beamed " I've done it, I've done it. I saved my passage I can go ... the next ship sails in 3 weeks. I have so much to do. Can we go tomorrow to the office? Mummy will you come with me to pay and het all the details? Isn't it exciting?...

Louis Armstrong's "What a wonderful world." song was playing on the radio and at that moment it was exactly that. Everyone was excited, the neighbours called round to share this news and a toast was raised. JR returned home and on hearing the commotion within by then with all the family circle and friends involved and now understood his first daughter's departure was imminent and congratulated her with a loving hug and a kiss on her forehead.

When dinner had finished John Richards called Lynette for one of their usual after dinner walks along the sea wall. His tone changed and he indicated to Lyn to sit on the bench by the bandstand as they watched the Atlantic oceans soft waves ebb and flow JR's facial expression showed his joy but his eyes were stern and definite, what followed was a speech about being obedient and diligent. Lynette could not have anticipated this next part...

JR's words stunned her, "I've thought about this a great deal and after careful consideration I have decided that you should not travel alone. It is England the Mother Country and a very long way overseas. We cannot help you from here, you need someone with you as a chaperone, someone we can trust. Lynette contemplated these words, could this be true, who could he mean still only when he said Nancy will be travelling with you next year so you will have time to save for her passage too, did the awful truth wash over her. This was a tsunami. They walked home in silence.

Beatrice gave her daughter sweet tea with a little rum in it to help her to get over the shock and deflation from the high notes of the afternoon. Lynette and Beatrice knew better than to rebuke JR as any decision made was law, still she tried but to no avail.

How Lynette cried huge salty tears drenching her bedclothes, there was no consoling her. The audacity of it was that she was the responsible one who would be chaperoned by Nancy the party girl irresponsible, irrepressible and impetuous one. Lynette would work hard, save and the pay for her passage, deferring hope ambitions and dreams all for Nancy who would not do her such a big favour.

Beatrice comforted her daughter Lynette, her 3rd pregnancy resulting in the first surviving child form JR. Nancy was from her first marriage which ended. She met John Richards and had a whirlwind romance, they married and they had suffered the traumatic death of their first-born twin boys. The twins had lived only 5 days born prematurely had little chance of survival, it was simply not their time. Financially they could never have afforded them so it was a cruel blessing that they left. Both exquisite and perfectly formed born at home they were simply too early, tiny and failed to thrive. Within a year Lynette was born, a girl child, strong and vital from the second she arrived she announced loudly that she was here to stay. Born in good times she would have a better life than the twins could have had, filled with chances.

As she contemplated the coming year the anguishes of the hurt and bitterness ebbed away to be replaced by a fervent determination to succeed and make the most of this extra time with her family. 1959 was only 12 months away, she convinced herself it would be a blessing to take her sister and she accepted the challenge. It was difficult when she saw the immense Dutch ship the Willemstad readied for passage on the day she would have been leaving at the dock for its 21-day voyage. She went up close and touched the vessel wishing it safe passage and promising she would be on the sister ship next year February, the sailors and deck hands were speaking different languages and hurried themselves as they walked on the ship. The local ladies of the night plied their wares in their highly painted faces and skin-tight clothing leaving little to the imagination as they laughed and joked while flashing their golden jewellery and gold teeth smoky smiles she was sure she recognised one as a former neighbour but did not stay to ask.

All manner of goods were being unloaded from British motor cars to cheeses like Old Amsterdam which was so old that it would crumble to the touch and was deliciously savoury. Salted cod fish, Raleigh and Batavus bicycles were being off loaded .

The Port was a wonderful place. Why punish yourself with these images and scenes she said to herself . It even crossed her mind not to go but to remain in British Guiana and Georgetown stay in the civil service, marry have children ...why go to such effort who was she to have such ambitions ...why save for Nancy Why?? So, it went on in her head ...but finally she resolved to do the right thing and go for it.

She prayed about it and Lynette decided to take a small holiday going by road on the bus to Dutch Guiana now called Suriname to visit the synagogue grandad George had visited in Paramaribo and give thanks and pray for success. She would also use the opportunity to visit and stay with her loving Aunt Josephine and her Dutch Guianese husband Oscar (which she spelt in her own style of "Okar") This was JR's little sister a hairdresser who had chosen to live in Dutch Guiana in the village of Nickerie just over the border. Lynette could take in the sights, recuperate and gain strength for the hard work ahead. It was just what she needed...

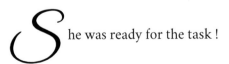

*S*he was ready for the task !

THE ORANJESTAD OCEAN LINER 1959

BERTH 2210 WITH PORTHOLE.

*W*hile deciding where to study nursing Lynette had checked the map of England noting the advice from Father Goodrich had advised Taunton Somerset stating it was the warmest part of England, so Lynette chose the Maudsley hospital in Taunton. She advised Nancy to choose Oxford about 150 miles away for her SRN training so freedom was in sight...no one had a map of England and the citizens envisaged everywhere was close like Georgetown and BV. Thus, they would travel together and part at the docks of Portsmouth to go in opposite directions to their end destinations. Without a map of England in the home not a soul would know until years later. The Mother Country was a place where distance was in a few miles not hundreds. So, Nancy would go to the esteemed John Radcliffe hospital in Oxford where she would continue to work for almost 50 years until her retirement.

Lynette liked this cunning plan. So much excitement nervous energy and wonder. The Oranjestad ship had returned to the Port of Georgetown to deliver good from England and the Islands and in return to collect like a bee gathering honey from flowers would harvest the brightest and finest youth of the colonies to bring back to the hive of the Mother countries of England and the Netherlands.

It was an immense ship with 4 funnels and some 8 decks some cabins had balconies and others large square windows but the cheaper £100 fare travellers had a porthole via which to see the approaching new world. She was a fine vessel clean spic and span, everything gleamed and sparkled . Nothing was out of place and the 3 berth cabins on the lower decks were like mini apartments. This was the first time Lynette had her own bed. There were 2 bunk-beds, then one single bed, a bathroom with w.c, shower and wash table they provided the soap and towel. The entirety was for their exclusive use. Space under the bed could be used for the grip-suitcases and the wardrobe made perfect use of the space. Carpeted throughout and exquisitely decorated, you could not tell it had been a former troop ship in 1939-1945 .

Plymouth Devon the final port of call for the 3 ladies, was well known for its maritime heritage, with its natural harbour and rich history. From here the Pilgrim fathers embarked for the new world of what is now USA in 1620 on the Mayflowers Ship. The town was hit hard by Nazi bombs in WWII as it was a strategic military target but it was now rebuilding and recovering.

The Oranjestad had exquisite public areas such as the vast dining rooms, plush gold curtains and highly patterned carpets throughout, especially custom-made crockery and all furniture had the logo of the ship. There was a radio room, theatre, cinema, casino, library and all manner of attractions to occupy the passengers on the twenty-one-day voyage.

These neophyte tourists were to be entertained night and day and when not sleeping they could eat as much as they pleased …Each day they would leave their homelands farther and farther behind.

The ship was more accustomed to high living, free spending guests who would think nothing of dropping 20% of the fare on gratuities but our British colonial passengers who had scrimped and saved for their place on board would give maximum £1…Most like Lynette made sure to get value for money and enjoyed breakfast, lunch and dinner and the many snacks and freebies given during the day. Such excess of provisions and types of dishes they had never seen.

Itinerary for the cruise was as follows Georgetown, British Guiana, Paramaribo, Dutch Guiana, Port of Spain, Trinidad, Funchal, Madeira, Portsmouth, England and the final destination of Amsterdam/Rotterdam Netherlands for the Dutch Guianese passengers. The trio would be leaving at Portsmouth. For all on board it was to be an adventure of a lifetime average age was 20 and for all it was the first-time they had ever been so far away from all they knew. It was an opportunity to see for the first time how others lived and they saw the poverty of the other islands long the way and always took extra food or prags so they could distribute the excess to the waiting hungry impoverished folk they met on disembarkation hovering around the ports.

The British Colonial Office had issued a list of items required for those that would emigrate. Beatrice had saved and bought all the items her girls needed. It was strange it was all imported from London and now would be returning there the irony was not lost. The grip or suitcase was a very expensive item and the God Parents gave this kind donation, Lynette's God Father Uncle Lim was a Chinese freemason Lodge member and a close friend of JR. He had chosen the elegant beige tartan design and painted L.E.R in white letters on the side so his Lyn could find it on arrival .Nancy had another style.

Everything was packed up and ready two days before and on Sunday Father Goodrich held a special service at the local church of St Sidwell's for everyone who was leaving and their families. St Georges was packed. Among the upbeat hymns and prayers for

Success, safe passage and good studies, John Augustus Richards asked the choir to sing his father-in-law George Browns favourite hymn that had had learnt in his sojourn in London. JR had by now had a grave understanding of the implications and the adventure before them and insisted that the sailor's hymn…"Eternal Father strong to save, for those in Peril on the Sea" be sung and it was.

At home after the service all the folk of Palm Street came to number 47 rum flowed and the party carried on till the wee hours.

One and all came by to see Nancy and Lynette and bless the intrepid pair as they were about to depart. Unsaid but definitely in their hearts was a young neighbour, a boy just 14 years old called Sydney Caleb one of 5 children whose father a wealthy plumber, had died the year before leaving the family in dire straits. All the community helped them with hand me down clothing and food packages. Mrs Caleb had become a wealthy lady with greater status through her husband's enterprises and thought herself of a far superior class to the rest of Palm Street...Her house was the fanciest in the street already a duplex it was chic with matching curtains and enviably shiny brass trimmings within the mahogany parlour furnished living area, which no common Palm Street resident was welcomed within. She no longer spoke or exchanged pleasantries with her neighbours. However, when her husband died suddenly the reality was that only through his endeavours were they able to maintain such a high standard of living and soon the stark truth was they were to go to the poor house. Prospects were reversed. Her daughters instead of marrying well chose to eke out a living within the world's oldest professions and went to make gold miners satisfied in Linden and the Port of Georgetown area. Mrs Caleb and her mother who had elephantiasis were left with Sydney and a younger baby brother they decided to make black pudding sausages for an income stream and they sold this every Saturday at home ...they were not above stealing a chicken from a neighbour to use in the savoury meat dish and blame the subsequent loss on a stray mongoose...Vincent and Owen were teased by Lynette when they bought Grandma Caleb's black pudding saying that she had made it from her excess fat in her swollen legs...

Well poor Sydney Caleb knew his family could not afford to send to him high school or technical college in Guiana, let alone overseas to study with such an expensive fare.

In Dick Whittington style he resolved to seek his fortune, get out of Guyana and help his Mother and Grandmother, since his whoring sisters had come to nought and lived day to day as drugged addicted women needing to smoking opium to carry out their profession, they cared for themselves only ...so taking a change of clothing and meagre rations in his backpack he smuggled himself onboard a ship. Nobody knew which vessel he chose. In his last note said he promised he would write when he arrived safely at a destination and he would send money to his mother but this was a year later and no correspondence had arrived or would ever be written or be delivered. It was presumed that he had squirrelled himself on board but that he never reached his destination maybe there was a ship wreck if he was thus presumed lost at sea. Palm Street mourned him and missed his jovial and helpful honest nature hence JR insisted on eulogising not only the positive aspects of the journey ahead but the realisation that not everyone made it.

It was so far; the photographer would accompany them to immortalise the last image of the family before they departed. Little did they know this was to be the last time the whole family would be under the same roof forever. The memories of Christmas 1958 with the traditional ham roast, imported chocolate and drunken delicious black cake with its divine white icing were simply that a memory. The new curtains traditionally put up to herald in the new year were still fluttering at the windows. JR had hired 3 taxis to take the whole family on the short ride to the port Palm street neighbours and Bourda Market traders came by wishing them well and bon voyage. Hugs galore and Hallelujahs all round. Even the local stray cats and dogs came by, knowing their regular scraps feeder was going away. Even sour face Murphy wished her well.

The Commemorative photographs taken that day would have to suffice as a lasting memorial for their loved ones until they would meet again, showed the fashion of the day with hats, gloves and handbags dresses for the ladies and hats and suits for the men. JR and Beatrice looked at their girls, how grown up they had become.

When had this happened, it was as though it was in a blink of an eye.

The whole family Brown from Beterverwagteng and Triumph came and as they all piled into the cars they spied straight ahead the funnels of the vessel that would carry their precious loved ones away from all they loved and knew.

Lynette was last to enter the car hovering at the door touching the brass number 47 that little Vincent had made and absorbing and photographing her home in her mind's eye committing to memory every detail. She was grateful now that she had enjoyed an extra year at home it was beyond worth in value. She then walked away bravely and entered in the vehicle.

At the port JR took charge. A porter was hailed and he met up with his lodge friend Mr Eustis the head of the Port and sorted out that the berth would be the best in its class, he promised he would sort everything out and he did. It was a given this is what the Freemasons did for each other. No harm would come to his precious children. Documentation was checked-all correct!

The family and friends admired the structure of the ship and although not permitted on board they could see it was an excellent chip. The sailors and crew were Dutch but they all spoke excellent English too.

Finally, time had arrived to leave and walk up the gangplank. Cuddles were given to last them till England lots of tears, strokes and wet kisses. They walked away courageously towards their destination. Once on-board ship they vied for a place at the dock railing to shout and wave to their families and ever so slowly the ship moved away. The anchor was raised and the ropes grasping the last tenuous links to their home removed.

The umbilical cord of the British Guiana landmass was severed.

They were off!

For a full 30 minutes they continued to stare in the direction of Georgetown the family familiar buildings and lights becoming ghosts before their eyes. They saw the villages and housing schemes disappear, then suddenly without warning the land was gone. Being below sea level, they had encountered for the first-time life at sea level and hence British Guiana had disappeared from view.

They went to their cabin and changed out of their Beatrice Richards Designed suits Peach coloured for Lynette and Blue for Nancy and put them safely away they would next be used in England. They donned regular casual clothes and went on to explore the ship together. In 2 days, they would arrive at Paramaribo Dutch Guiana, what an adventure.

Back in Georgetown a deflated Richards family and the Brown family had returned home almost silently each quietly praying and encapsulating the memories they had just made. The next 3 weeks they would be mentally calculating where the girls would be on the voyage, already they knew that the first stop was Paramaribo.

Always when a vessel departed with the cream of the talent of a nation it was as though a biblical rapture had occurred. The vanishing young people left gapping holes in their families and communities, markets and hearts. The next week the cathedral was missing 300 young people. Practical stuff like shopping in the market, something Lynette had always done was now Beatrice's task. The Seamstress may have been the wife of the Chief of the Market but she had no idea how to negotiate or haggle for the best prices ...also she now had to clean and tidy too. Sister Hilda helped out there as this she loved. But it was the mischievous sprightly Vincent and quiet soft-spoken Owen who missed her cheerfulness at home. JR brave as ever thought his heart would break if he cried so just quietly he prayed daily for good news and safety for them.

The cruise arrived at Paramaribo where they disembarked to look around and then sailed onwards towards Port of Spain and Trinidad, which unfortunately had a violent reputation so Nancy now suddenly being big sister forbade Lynette to leave the ship to explore. She would return later on the same ship and then Lyn would visit Trini. After that days and nights at sea, the endless board games, theatre skits, books to read and walk son deck until at last land was spotted at Madeira they were arriving at Funchal.

Every person got off ... Lynette bought a traditional typical hat as a souvenir and listened attentively to the new languages that she heard. Seeing the mountains and fantastic landscape soaking it all in , once past Madeira the Oranjestad continued further into Europe and England along the way the Captain would inform them of the various countries that they were passing along the way.

It was so far Plymouth Devon England was in sight, everyone

crammed the deck to watch, it was February now and awfully cold. Twenty first day was a great relief for Daphne who had been sharing the third berth in the cabin with the sisters. Daphne had been sea sick since embarkation in Georgetown and was now stick thin but grateful to be on dry land. She had earnt her sea legs.

Disembarkation meant that Lynette and Nancy would part ways. Daphne was collected by her brother. Nancy got her train to Reading then onto Oxford and Lynette was collected and taken to the steam train to London and on to Norbury passing through Clapham Junction which was at the time the busiest station in the world .She would stay in Norbury to stay a few weeks at the home of Father Goodrich's parents . A reciprocal gesture in response to Beatrice and John Richards kindness to their only son Derek's favourable treatment and the warm hospitality shown when this middle-aged couple more used to going to Bognor Regus on vacation ventured out to British Guiana on the same cruise liner to see their son in situ in Guyana.

Lynette saw for the first time the famous River Thames a spritely but narrow body of water which was at least 20 times smaller than the demerara river but had at that time already over ten bridges to cross over and the Demerara River none.

The Goodrich's home in Norbury was on Strathyre Avenue a truly delightful address and a warm home. Pretty tree lined pavements and terraced homes all kept perfectly with prize blooms and rose bushes and neatly clipped lawns to the front and vegetable patches and flowers for the house beautification at the rear. Lynette got a bedroom at the front of the house and had an eiderdown and blankets. Mrs Goodrich also gave her a winter coat. Ice formed at the window and as she breathed smoke arose so cold was it. Uncle Charlie had advised Lyn to acclimatise for the cold by putting her hand in the fridge ...this was no match. 2 weeks flew by and she was off to Somerset, each subsequent visit to London she was able to stay with them, they treated her as their own daughter.

Paddington station steam trains chugged in and puffed out travelling on a 2nd class ticket to Taunton watching the English countryside unfurling outside. On arrival Matron welcomed the new intake group and introduced the future nurses to their dormitories. It was not just Caribbean also Irish and English young people came to learn and serve. Here Lynette would stay for 3 years going from zero knowledge to near perfection in her clinical studies both practical and theoretical. This was the start of an illustrious career.

She would receive a monthly salary net of Nine British Pounds … £9:00 per month .

The many deductions were for her future pension, superannuation, room and board, uniform and sundries. From this paltry sum she sent remittances of £5:00 each month home to her parents. Over the years it increased incrementally as her skills and ability grew .One day when Lynette would be offered early retirement at aged 56 from the NHS she would realise the small deductions started paying for he future pension all those years ago and smile. From this £9:00 salary the £5:00 sent by Lynette, JR and Beatrice rebuilt 47 Palm Street to make it 100% bigger home by making the stilted clapboard house into a two-story house as it is today .

JR was so proud of his little girl.

LYNETTE AND NANCY GOING
LEAVING GUYANA TO GO TO
LONDON THE LAST PICTURE
BEFORE BOARDING THE
ORANGESTAD

LA BONNE INTENTION SUGAR PLANTATION CLOSES

The Mass Exodus circa 1962

*L*a Bonne Intention became Les Misérables for the folk who worked on the sugar plantations who were already on short time part time work the last day came when the order books closed off totally and no new markets could be found for the sugar. Unfortunately, sugar prices continued to decline and even the trademark name of Demerara Sugar could not hold its own on the world markets. The whole industry in BV was no longer viable. Mass unemployment ensued and it was now that others who could would leave their homes just as the younger ones had done earlier.

Hilda, Pauline and Beryl and their respective families would all leave for America and Canada.

Pauline had the misfortune to be married to the most unfaithful man in B.V. mister Walter David the "village ram" who was a stacker at the LBI plantation and part time pig farmer in Hog Sty. She had worked as a shorthand typist in the legal department of the LBI Estate company. They both lost their jobs money was tight.

Hilda was Lynette's favourite aunt because she was genuinely kind and had a super loving nature. No scholar she loved any kind of practical or physical manual work like cleaning and washing clothes and such like. She also lost her job at LBI, but lucky for her the at the American Atkins Airforce Base she was able to find work with the Goldstein's a pilot family with the air force. Here she cared for their home on the base and looked after the children. They were due to return as he had gained promotion to Captain in Washington DC so their time in sunny British Guiana was to end. As she was so good with the children the Goldstein's applied to request if Hilda could return to USA with them naturally Hector her good for nothing lazy, demanding, sloth of a husband would accompany her there.

Hector Thomas and Hilda had 2 children Gloria and George her 4-year younger brother. Hector had difficulty staying awake due to his lazy nature, still he was lucky he got a job as a prison guard in the Camp Street Prison in Georgetown through his father's connections and largesse. Father Thomas was a wealthy man with five houses in Hadfield Street which he rented out and he allowed Hector and Hilda to live on one rent free. A prison guard was relatively relaxed post, safe and secure his father a senior guard had enabled him to get the position…Simple work too with uniform, status and benefits, pension plan. Just checking on the inmates ensuring their welfare and that they do not escape! Hector resigned 3 times stating the work life balance was too taxing for him …simply patrolling the jail house, opening and closing the cell doors all too much for the idle man. Indeed, even walking was too much he delighted in jumping on the broad shoulders of Hilda back and getting a piggy back to save himself from any extra exertion. Lynette and the Richards family loathed him. He had a slothful mentality and Hilda being a Brown was the opposite. Daughter Gloria was a lovely caring girl who would go on to be a nurse in America and George was a sweet, honest little boy who was openly effeminate he enjoyed playing with the girls and their toys boys would tease him and pick on him calling him names like ante-man and sissy he suffered. He was cute and loved by all the family. Now with Hector again out of work and his father losing patience with his wayward son it was a no brainer to uproot the Thomas Family all on the one immigration visa and a one-way flight to Washington DC. It was the kind of opportunity that could make such a difference to their future. Surely even Hector would find employment and the family would prosper.

And so, it was that the family of Hector and Hilda boarded the large cargo plane and reached for the distant land which they were to call home within hours. They were the first in the family to go on a plane . On arrival Hector was d.o.a ,he loved Washington DC and the American lifestyle. A routine started which was not to change for the next 40 years Hector would walk the 100 yards weather permitting to accompany Hilda to catch the first of 3 busses she needed to take in order to get to the Goldstein's home across town. He would then buy a newspaper and take to his "La Z boy chair" and watch his tv shows all day until she came home, after the dinner was made by Hilda he would eat in his chair and snooze. They lived in a nice home which she bought it was in the NW district and black working-class area. Her sweet nature meant she never would complain, always grateful and enthusiastic, rain hail, snow sunshine she went to work . Her American dream did not include Disneyland, Grand Canyon tours or Florida sun shine vacations just work. She would arrive in time to make breakfast for the family, then lunch and set up things for dinner, basically she cared for the families every need and in turn they cared for her.

Hector was visited by the Jehovah Witnesses on the doorstep preaching and found religion and became a Jehovah Witness and converted the whole family and then promptly left the belief as fellowship was too far away. But Hilda held on fast to the creed and was a serious devotee and natural follower.

Hector would never work a day in his life in USA his best friend was the TV remote control. The children became US citizens and they never returned to British Guiana as a family, it was simply out of their reach, they attended and graduated high school and subsequently entered the work force.

By chance and fortune because of Hilda's exemplary work ethics and service she was asked if she could recommend a family member to work for another family so in this way she was able to introduce

Pauline to the airbase and soon Pauline and Walter were on their way to Washington. Pauline would leave BV where she was highly qualified but unable to find suitable work to do child care and Walter the pig farmer became a night watchman.

The work was bearable but to a bright lady like Pauline it was clear Hilda had omitted to mention the Jim Crow laws and the racism whereby black people were fighting for civil rights …She hated the racism she encountered USA though loved the people and country and thus started saving to leave immediately… she sent word back home and warned Beryl not to come there.

Beryl the youngest sister would also leave with her only son Pat (Patrick) and her head master teacher husband Cyril who had been offered a position to teach in North Carolina…heeding Sister Pauline's advice they accepted the job offered up North in Canada teaching specifically in Canada. Cyril worried rightly that going from complete freedom to an apartheid state of affairs would be traumatic and degrading. He was right, Hilda handled the atrocities of her life by securing her future in heaven. Hectors small narrow world was his living room "Stanford and Son"," The price is right!" were his world. The house deteriorated around him a small repair would be left until it became major and after 40+ years of just sitting comfy the city hall declared the place uninhabitable and it was so condemned. Hilda finally retired and ended her days in a nursing home which she loved it was the first time she was cared for her grandchildren Sonia, Michelle, Edward and Anthony took care of her until her time came. They left Hector to fend for himself and he too was placed in a home but this was a government home and very basic he died soon after and got a $50-dollar state cremation plan.

Gloria became a hard-working dedicated nurse, married to Edward and had the 4 children. She succumbed to cancer which was treatable but due to the need to have blood transfusions which was not permitted due to her devoted Jehovah Witness beliefs it spread further than it should have done and she died young at age 48.

Pauline and Walter stayed in the USA for the allotted 4 years of their visa and then returned to BV in Guyana and freedom of home

.They hoped that the now independent Guyana would be a land of opportunity where you did not need to leave to make a crust to eat or have a chance to excel. They had found the blatant legal racial discrimination too much to bear, the "Yes Ma'am" stuck in her throat and separations of the services to the races such as in a restaurant etc too much. Economically they would not be better off but freedom costs so they returned home.

Beryl cared for her son Pat who went on to become a nurse. Beryl would establish a nursery school at home and Cyril became instead of a Head Master, a regular teacher of English in a local Hamilton high school. They lived in Hamilton Ontario and had a good life. Beryl was to have 4 grandchildren from Pat and his wife including Kevin who was her favourite. Out of all the sisters Beryl was the wealthiest. She returned each year to Guyana and was best place economically with property in Guyana and Canada. Only thing was that she had to endure the cold. Cyril died some 30 years ago but Beryl celebrated her 100th birthday with great gratitude and with all her Canadian family with her in her luxury nursing home in January 2019 and is with us still.

So, it was that Beatrice "lost" her sisters one by one and became lonesome without her daughters only Vincent and Owen remained. Every family in the land knew someone who was abroad. Ina few short years the missed ones were now a normalcy in every family and everyone awaited the postman's knock for the blue airmail envelope bringing the latest news .the Birthday cards and regular letters would contain valuable money ,hard currency £'s and $'s all was welcome. There was always someone missing for every family event or gathering an emptiness so real that it ached.

When the missing children began to marry total strangers thousands of mile away only camera shutter of the photographer could witness the split-second smile to proclaim the marriage had occurred. No Mother to make a dress and assure the young bride, no Father to give his daughter away or to check the groom out. In the spirit they would be there and they would make a feast in Georgetown and take a picture so that could be sent and added to the wedding album. There would be black cake, meats, rice, patties, fudge all manner of drink and the smiles would convey the heart felt congratulations.

The Guianese family members remaining in the homeland would hold a party and send a picture of them celebrating a thousand miles away to let them know they were with the newly wedded couple in spirit. No one could afford to send money to attend they could only dream and imagine the scene and send a telegram. So many disconnected grandchildren were born and baptized in the new world without grandparents and aunts, uncles, brothers or sisters in attendance and so it was. Absence was a terrible thing. Gone were the close family ties and the ever-reliable sources of honest advice and love that came with the old society.

Those at LBI Estate who had no such opportunities to travel to find other work languished in the mediocracy of their lives and would get odd jobs in the rice fields or would try other plantations to try to find work but most remained unemployed and thus poor. Few were lucky like Charlie who was able to work in the D'Aguilar rum Factory making molasses the life blood of the drink.

Times changed and British Guiana would never be the same again.

The Brain Drain had begun and it would prove to be unstoppable …eventually 700,000 Guyanese and their descendants would leave home and hence there are just as many citizens outside as there are inside. Everyday someone leaves…

Pauline at work in North Carolina, America

A new TV the fruits of her labour.

La Bonne Intention Gates with Sugar cane Motif.

Sugar Cane Fields La Bonne Intention Plantation.

© George Thomas
George Thomas served in The US Navy on a Submarine as an officer
during the
Vietnam War

CHARLIE BROWN AND MARY

*C*harlie Brown the only son of George and Queenie Brown was a fine figure of a man,
7 feet tall with a hand span of 12 inches. Giant Muscular man but really very quiet, shy, discreet and of few words like his mother...a smiled "aha" or "mmm" was as much as would say most days outside the family circle.

So, when it came to girls and a wife Queenie advised her son to marry Mary Doherty. Although she already had a daughter Annie, she was alone and struggling as the father of Annie had left so Charlie would be able to provide a perfect family.

Obedient Charlie did exactly this and married Mary adopting little Annie when she was just 4 years of age. Mary then bore him 2 children a boy and a girl and on his foreman wages they were able to live well. Then Mary went rouge presenting not one but five bastard children for the Ganga smoking Rastafarian man of the village. Charlie gentle as ever just cared for then as if they were his own even though everyone knew whose children they really were he allowed them all to carry his name. He understood that under the law the married man had to accept the children as his and more than this the Rastafarian man would not take care of them in any way and they would become ostracised from society. Charlie saw them as innocents and Charlie was more apt to caress and give a helping hand than to fight.

With LBI closed Charlie had also thought of emigrating with his family to USA but been rebuffed due to a cataract being diagnosed over his Left eye... so he would not at present pass the medical tests for the entry visa until it was corrected. Once it was done this painfully shy man would bravely be ready to leave all he knew and take his entire family to America ...the land of the free. It was planned to go there for a maximum of five years and return wealthy enough to set up and buy some land to build a bigger home without any debt and live happily in their old age.

All had been perfect he had 20/20 vision but somewhere around the birth of the second bastard child his sight became occluded. Maybe a physical embodiment of his heart not wishing him to see the reality of his marriage. Still he continued to work hard and was silent. He had made an agreement on his wedding day for richer or poorer, in sickness and health for better for worse and so on.

His reputation as an excellent worker preceded him and he was one of the few fortunate ones offered a deputy foreman job up river to help produce the molasses for the famous Rum which was not only given as a rum ration for the navy but also was exported all over the colonial realm. This was a modernised factory so fewer hands were needed so he felt fortunate only 40 men were needed to do the work of 400... but it was not certain. USA was a real job offer, but he would wait a while. The job would require him to do meticulous administration and so he needed the eye operated on to have a chance.

Georgetown hospital a sprawling Colonial wooden building was in the heart of the city. The Dray cart driven by Ponies were used as ambulances for the poorer only the wealthy travelled by one of the few motorised ambulances. A quick uneventful pleasant train journey traversing through the colourful little hamlets and villages gaily along the way. You could see clearly the distinction of a Hindu home from the triangular flags outside. There was for the most part harmony between the races especially in BV where mixture was the norm creating beautiful people, purity is not always pretty. He could see far out to the magnificent Ocean and the 280-mile fortified Dutch engineered dyke designed by Dhr Hora .T. Siccama Eng., construction had started in 1855 and was completed by convict labour in 1874 and this amazing piece of engineering had been keeping the city and country safe for so many years.

Arrival at the hospital public areas one saw all manner of sickness and tragedy, one had to remind oneself that these were the lucky ones. The room filled with pregnant ladies, people with sniffing children, elephantiasis, machete injuries, cancers etc. Lepers had to stay in a secluded territory and were not allowed in town with out their obligatory bell chiming to all to stay away. There was a boy about 13 years old, Michael he was brought in on the dray cart ambulance, he had been hunting in the interior of the country with his father and had been the victim of a grievous miscalculation, his father had shot him in his leg thinking him a wild animal from afar.

They were an Amerindian family not used to the city and it was feared the leg could not be saved due to the devastating force of the shot gun's aim, Charlie felt for the boy and gave him a piece of fudge and dried his tears. It later transpired the injury was so serious well beyond the abilities of the provincial hospital that the only solution was to amputate above the knee .Michael was the youngest patient at that time to receive a prosthetic limb, he now works at a rehabilitation centre in Georgetown and runs marathons with his leg and wins.

Back to Charlie Brown after a 3 hour wait he was invited into the small office to see the Doctor wearing his white coat with half rim glasses perched on his nose and an arrogant authoritative air about him. "Charlie Brown cataract Left eye ...oh yes very straightforward we can fix that for you come back in 10 days Dr Castillo is coming in from Cuba and you can go his list. That is, it the nurse will give you the list you need to bring with you, the stay is about 5-10 days and after that you are good to go." He smiled and shook Charlie's all enveloping hand. Charlie was reassured.

Ten days later he had stayed overnight at Beatrice's home and enjoyed a delicious meal and a good game of Dominos with John and friends the night before, it was good to be among loved ones his children had given him a picture to keep with him as a good luck charm Mary wished him well but was now with her worthless Rastafarian man... while the cat's away...

They walked to the hospital it was Friday 13th Beatrice read his stars ...it was not great but she did not tell him. Kissing him farewell "See you later!" he answered and "I will see you too he beamed." They prayed for success.

JR booked Charlie in and unpacked his belongings there was a snack for after wards as the hospital treatment did not include meals. They also brought their own sheets.

The 10 days had gone quickly and he had absorbed all the sights he could the defunct sugar cane fields statuesque and elegant swaying in the breeze. The children playing in the sandy dusty streets, Brown's corner, young lovers paddling their homemade rafts along the canals, the cockers, small wooden bridges, the stray dogs who loved everyone regardless of pedigree, his sisters his home. He was ready. Pauline and Beatrice set out his clothes and readied him. JR went to Bourda Market.

Dr Castillo was a small old Cuban man with a thick Spanish accent he had volunteered to come to Guiana but in reality, he was already regretting it as his wife had that morning been found in bed with a black man and he wanted revenge and to add to his woes he had been fired from his job in Cuba Havana hospital due to incompetence and the head of the hospital had been a Black man Professor Jonathan. Dr Castillo had faked his references, he was out for revenge.

The Left eye was marked for the operation. Dr said no "Lado Drecho." The nurse handed him the notes LEFT not RIGHT . "Ah Okay, Sie." He had anaesthetic and was counting backwards ... The Cuban doctor Castillo started his work .

In 43 minutes, the lens was removed and Charlie was returned to the ward to recover.

On the fifth day anticipation mounted and all the family came to see the results. Doctor Castillo came too and did the honours .

" There you are !" Tell me what you can see ,how many fingers am I holding up, He looked at the audience of family smiling ...Beatrice noticed that his Right eye looked swollen and asked why ...? No need to wait for an answer from the good doctor. Charlie said "It's worse I can't see anything now...."

Slowly the family realised that their darling Charlie Brown was now completely blind. Dr Castillo had removed the good eye's functioning lens and rendered him as Samson after Delilah had shorn the Nazarene's hair. How they wept . The Police were called the doctor was placed in jail pending trial and was eventually sent to the Mad house for the rest of his days. Charlie was not alone in total the Doctor destroyed 15 people's lives by rendering them either partially or completely blind.He was sent to the jungle mad house to live with snakes and rats in squalor...he went totally crazy. Charlie Brown would never be able to work again or live independently...had it not been for his Richards and Brown family he would have had a begging bowl and had to fend for himself on the streets of Georgetown.

Mary never one to let a marital vow bind her soon left him to emigrate to America with all the children she was to remain there and lived with her children till age 92 and Charlie's real children his two children Ossie and Nancy became a dentist and lawyer respectively. She Mary was to become a preacher woman always with her bible close at hand. The Rastafarian man's children fared worse but still better than they may have done had they remained in Guyana. The Brown and Richards family would never forgive Mary's abandonment of their brother Charlie in his hour of need after all he had done for her.

Aunt Pauline and Walter came back permanently from USA to take care of business, America had been a good economic move. Walter was to keep pigs to sell and breed and made a good living with this trade. They also won a sweep stake and were able with this money to modify the house so that Charlie could live easier they would care for him for the rest of his life... when I saw him last I was

21 and he was sitting in his usual space a position by the wide-open windows a calm breeze touching his face. Eyes wide open as though he was able to watch the children at play outside in the street and yards below. Listening to the cockerel and farmyard sounds. He never got the chance to learn braille or get a guide dog all the usual things that one can do in Europe when faced with blindness enabling one to have a better life and adjust to their new reality .

He lived in this way for some 19 years he did not see his black hair had become grey. Within him he was ready to go but he was to wait a while. Beryl and Cyril came back to BV for Christmas from cold Canada with Kevin, her grandson. The Christmas presents were readied and the cooker was busy with cakes and all manner of fantastic food. Charlies biological children also came to stay over for the Christmas period it was his best time ever. He laughed and smiled until it ached his face JR and Beatrice came too it was a real opportunity for them all to have fellowship and share the love.

He retired to his room and slept quietly oh so quietly his breath ever softer until he decided it was enough and asked to be with God his prayer was answered and on Boxing day they found his lifeless body. His sprit was released and could now oversea all around him the flowers the family that loved him the grandchildren everything was now visible and it was good.

He remained unassuming, quiet and softly spoken, one wonders how he really felt.

I believe he was grateful to God that the last faces he saw and could recall were that of his family his sisters and brother in law JR

He was buried in the family plot at St Mary's the Virgin Beterverwagteng with Queenie and George his parents and he was now safe and sound no one could ever harm him again. Rest in Peace Shalom Uncle Charlie.

Charlie was a great gentleman.

"I AM GOING TO LONDON TO SEE HER MAJESTY THE QUEEN."

circa 1962

*L*ynette Richards was summoned to the Matron's office. Her best friend Bernadette an Irish student from County Laoise in Eire straightened her nurses cap and wished her luck as it was usually for a telling off… "Fingers crossed its good news."

Lyn ran quickly and with much trepidation knocked on the door " Enter " Matron a slim attractive woman in starched blue uniform in her mid 40's, invited her in and bade her to be seated. There was an envelope on the desk addressed to Miss Lynette E. Richards … " We have not opened it as it is addressed to you with strictly personal on it and it's from the Lord Chamberlain's office….so you can open it here, I am responsible for your welfare after all." At this moment a senior doctor and another nurse entered to observe the opening of the envelope.

"We want you to open it Now...!" Dr Willis said.

"So, I am not in trouble." Lynette answered.

"NOT AT ALL…OPEN IT." They cried.

Lynette opened the envelope and an embossed stiff white card with golden letters and the royal crest emerged. An invitation has been extended from HRH HM Queen Elizabeth II to Miss Lynette E. Richards to attend a Royal Garden Party at Buckingham Palace in London. It was to be in 2 months. An instruction on the dress code was given along with a badge to wear on the day, one guest was permitted. She knew she would take her best friend, Bernadette.

The invitation was in recognition of her achieving the highest ever recorded marks consistently for her studies not only practical but also theory. She was also to be presented with 2 huge books on clinical nursing which were a very highly valued prize. It was a celebration to showcase the brightest and the best of the colonies and to represent British Guiana and to give incentive to the scheme that Mr Enoch Powell MP Minister of Health had introduced was working perfectly. Lynette had consistently attained 99%-100% in her exams.

Matron beamed and actually hugged Lynette, "Oh my dear you have done us proud. Well done!"

Everyone was pleased. That afternoon in celebration everyone was given a slice of Victoria sponge cake... Lynette considered her three years training, all the hard work and hardship had been worth it ...the Christmas dinner of the solitary boiled egg, the month of being the bedpan queen where she was responsible for cleaning and stacking the soiled bedpans and making them shine again, the long walks to work from the dormitories over a mile away because of no money for bus fare as she was sending over half her paltry salary home, and the constant double duty of studies and practical patient caring ...she had actually Loved it. Finally, she had recognition that she did it good...and then from Royalty.

Bernadette was waiting outside. "So, "Pocket Piece" what's happening ?"The nick name had been given when on her 21st birthday a long-awaited birthday card had arrived from home Georgetown, but only the card saying Love and best wishes from Mummy, Daddy and the home circle, no little dollar bill, and she had wailed "On my 21st Birthday and no pocket piece enclosed!" the other students had not heard of this tradition of money in the card and the name stuck.

A telegram was sent to Guyana and of course JR and Beatrice could not have been prouder the whole of her world heard about it on the radio the papers and of course in Palm Street too. At the office above Bourda Market John Richards looked at his sovereigns' picture and thought how unique it was that his little girl would be meeting HRH HM the Queen of England and the Royal Family of colonies and he bowed in awe of this privilege to befall his family.

Beatrice went to the best and only department store in British Guiana, Bookers on Regent Street and bought material for the dress. She would design it and send it from British Guiana to her daughter in Taunton...only the very best would do no market material for the Royal Garden Party.

The great day arrived she left the Goodrich's home with Bernadette and they went together to Victoria station and then a short walk to the Palace they were dressed with hat and gloves and the practised their courtesies to each other. All the other great students from the colonies were there invitation in hand they walked through the gates observing the guards in their uniforms with shiny golden buttons. There was so much to see the gardens were so pretty and the people beautiful and from all over the realm.

HRH Her Majesty Queen Elizabeth II accompanied by HRH Prince Philip were heralded and the National anthem was played everyone stood to attention. After which the Queen gave a short welcoming speech was made and thanked the guests for their acceptance for leaving their homes to come to help England. They were congratulated on their outstanding performance.

Tea time ,cake scones with fresh cream, sandwiches and gallons of tea. It was a chance to chat and mingle. there was the line up and the time came when Lynette would be introduced Bernadette made sure she was perfect. The officer introduced her to the Queen announcing her achievements as described on the receiving her card ...

Your majesty this is Miss Lynette Richards from British Guiana and she has done outstandingly well in all her exams to become an SRN. Lynette curtsied perfectly and beamed, as Her Majesty gloved hand was extended in welcome so she got to shake hands too.

"Welcome to England Are you enjoying Somerset ? It is beautiful there Where are your parents living in British Guiana . Oh,

Georgetown delightful the Garden City ...well keep up your good work and no doubt you will enjoy a successful career, enjoy yourself. Thank you for coming ."

It was over all too soon and the iconic picture of Mummy beaming outside the palace went back to 47 Palm street and JR got another copy which he placed in his office just under the portrait of his Queen.

All that training had been worth it for this one day she had learnt so much, seen so much, births, deaths, raw emotions of anguish and joy. Lyn cared for patients, cleaned patients, dealt with scorn and discrimination and travelled a world away from those she held dear and the land she loved to serve in the NHS.

She was to continue her excellence passing her exams and graduating top in her class.

A prize a silver buckle for the nurse's uniform was given as tradition by the parents but poor Lynette would not have this present until many years later. After passing all her exams she was Registered as a State Registered Nurse. It was official. Lynette had managed to save up enough to buy a return ticket to Home to see everyone and so she embarked on the long 21-day trip again...this time she would disembark in Trinidad which big sister Nancy had previously forbidden due to fears over safety and she appreciated the calypso music and the beauty of the Island. She loved it .

At the dock side in Georgetown the whole family attended they had arrived a full 2 hours before the ship would dock to get their first glimpse of their precious child. It was good to be home. As before the subsea land mass suddenly appeared there was British Guiana ...so good to be home 47 Palm street had been polished to within an inch of its life and was standing like a palace 2 stories high in white washed excellence...

Her little salary in English Pounds had helped build this now 4-bedroom home two storey home, a truly remarkable achievement. Days were spent reminiscing explaining , sharing eating fruits long not seen in England like mangos and soursop. Visiting friends including Miss Elaine at the Ministry of Health and family. Travelling

on the steam locomotive train and simply soaking up the sunshine…
the days were gone all too quickly. From what JR understood he saw
the future for his sons Owen and Vincent to be in England and the
plan was made for them too to join the many leavers. He could see the
tremendous unemployment and underemployment coming and he
was right.

Few returned Lynette was one these few. Her dedication and
devotion to her parents would endure always. JR gave her advice as
she must now choose to specialise, he advised midwifery always a fan
of Moses story he said you will always have work. And so, it was that
Lynette applied to Birmingham University hospital to do her state
Registered Midwifery Training. She would contribute the fares of
Owen and Vincent and they too would come to study and work in
England both would become successful Electrical Engineers. JR saw
electricity was going to become common and said they must learn all
about it.

Lynette flew back on British Airways DC10 to London Gatwick
Airport from the newly built airport at Temerhri British Guiana.

By the way an aside about our Lynette "Pocket Piece" when she got
home she not only had a wonderful 21st birthday party but she
received a gold chain with key specially made in Guiana gold with 21
in key form for her coming of age birthday.

TRAINING IN TAUNTON

Lynette Richards outside Buckingham Palace with fellow winners in the dress that Mummy Beatrice made for her and sent from British Guiana to Taunton Somerset.
circa 1962 © Lynette Richards-Lorde

Newspaper articles with Lynette .

© Lynette Richards-Lorde

Time off in Taunton.1961 © Lynette Richards-Lorde

Lynette Richards-Lorde returns to Taunton 2016. © Ruthy Richards-Levi

MRS LYNETTE EVANGELINE BABALOLA

*P*rince Olawuji Babalola son of the Chief hailed from Ekiti State Nigeria, had decided to marry a Caribbean nurse. They were pretty, innocent, clever and reliable earners. He was a qualified Accountant after all and he could do the math.

Unable to attain work in accountancy he rented out property, buying them and enabling those affected by the notices stating No Irish, No Blacks, No dogs to pay an astronomical amount to him for accommodation. He had been in England to study for the bar at Middle temple but his studies had eluded him …Why work and study when rental collection was so much simpler and pure profit? He observed that the nurses were as a rule diligent and hard working. He had a false leg after a botched operation but he never let that hinder him. Olawuyi also had quite a past which someone like JR could have easily found out about but that was to remain hidden from his chosen prey for many a year, our Lynette.

The invitation to come to the Mother country and study and work had been heard all over the Empire with people coming from as far as New Zealand, India and Canada… so it was a short trip for those coming from Africa. The African's and Caribbean's were thus brought together via the Colonial office edit in London. England was the land of opportunity the place to become the best you can be a nurse, doctor, engineer, lawyer or just help out by working on the underground, post office or the buses...

Some 400 years after slavery had forced African's to be ripped away from their birth places, their languages to toil in far off unknown destinations...these Caribbean descendants were to prove by their very existence the theory of osmosis within their DNA that they were the best of the best. They were still standing! Having survived the long marches to the coastal ports from the jungle forests in the interior regions, they then endured captivity in the cages and dungeons at the holding bays.

Once ships were ready they were the cargo in the bowels of the ship chained and shackled the lay in their own filth on wooden planks. On arrival they were sold to harsh slave masters and endured punishing regimes on the plantations. Families were sold as individuals so separation was inevitable. Uneducated except in the New Testament to expect reward in a nether region as yet undiscovered or proven. These people lost so much not only family, customs, language, land, wealth and all possessions but they also lost their most treasured possession Freedom.

Once they realised that they had effectively been sold down the river they got to grips with the situation and those who had survived all the above had the slim chance to learn the new language of their slave masters, adjust to the accommodation and learn on job, whether that was on the cotton fields of America or sugar plantations of the Caribbean. Those who could make it would eventually have offspring who would be Free.

They were fortunate not to be in a culture where the men would be castrated routinely as occurred in some countries to the East but in the West, they were treated more as commodities and were encouraged to procreate and so provide more free workers. Not that they got the choicest cuts of meat on which to thrive ...The chicken and pig innards, pig snouts, salted pig tails chicken feet, salt beef and cat fish were the cast-off throw away food that became the delicacies they relished and these are now today staples in the diet. They became as superhuman as in spite of all they endured they strode forward with gusto .

It was these innocent descendants of these slaves who now were to meet with their African counterparts…Little did they realise that many of these incredibly wealthy individuals from the African continent had gained wealth via the slave trade and their progenitor were the prima facie reason for their ancestor's capture and enslavement !

Olawuyi would boastfully say "We made money out of you twice, first we sold you as slaves and now you are free you need housing and we are the only ones who will accept you in our houses…Life is good."

In search for love they would mistakenly believe with the similarities in colour the Africans were the same as the Caribbean folk. It was assumed the Africans language and their older cultural heritage would add gravitas to the Caribbean's shallow family tree which usually only went back as far the Grandparents. The exotic names rolled off the tongue and had meanings. Babalola means wealth of the father, this in comparison to their slave owner names like David, Thomas, Richards and the like. It was a chance to return to their roots. Some like Prince Olawuyi had the extra bonus of a royal linage, so attractive. So, they married these unknown entities and had solitary weddings with no close family members, no parental advice or support and no introductions or welcomes to the new in laws, a strange way to be in union and hoped it was going to be a fairy tale romance.

Lynette had her doubts as to whether he was the one for her especially when they argued over the manner he had inherited his fortune … she called it blood money. Unfortunately, he forced his way with her and I am the result. She was totally devastated and booked a passage home to Daddy.

Olawuyi was not her knight in shining armour nor would he ever be and she wanted out. Arriving at 47 Palm Street the ever-ready photographer captured us in his studio.

JR and Beatrice took control. He listened carefully to the whole situation and after a long pause he poured out some rum and chased it with coconut water with ice. Lynette, he served just coconut water no rum, Beatrice sat on her chair next to him….that was her answer to her right there in the glass. He said this child is ours. This child is a Richards first and fore most you as the mother must do all you can to stay healthy this may be your only opportunity to have a child and this baby is ours and is welcome. If things get difficult for you send the child to us I am retiring soon so we will as Richards Family along with all of us in Palm Street we will take care of her. Everything will be well…but you must first return and marry this man. This child will be legitimate no matter what… he is a ***** but maybe he has given us the greatest gift of all, think of how many countless ancestor's we have lost because of their family's dastardly deeds and now this happens …well we accept.

Final photograph taken before Lynette would leave Palm Street on De Orangestad Ship L-R Lynette, JR, Vincent, Beatrice and Owen.

Displeased with the advice but ever obedient Lyn returned in July and on 14th November 1964 she married my father in a registry office wedding the proof photographs were sent showing to 47 Palm Street as evidence of the legality of the doomed nuptials. Mrs Babalola can be seen unsmiling in a black and white picture in a grey suit seated with her new husband the Prince of Battersea, Olawuyi Babalola Prince of Ekiti State Nigeria grinning beside her. She never met her in laws, it was strictly a London affair. No pictures were ever ordered .

The couple would live at 2 Stockwood Avenue (now demolished)Battersea, London's shady side of town at that time grim and grey. The stresses of living with Olawuyi and the pregnancy led to Lynette getting hypertension and there was a serious chance of life-threatening Pre-eclampsia. Lynette would have to spend the rest of the pregnancy monitored and in bed rest in hospital. Ever mindful of status and ambitious she resolved to take herself across town to the countryside of Hillingdon Uxbridge one of the best hospitals and a good address to put on a birth certificate. A whole month early on the 15th December 1964 at 18:00 a tiny innocent bundle of mischief was born ... She shared the birthday with her Uncle Vincent and his subsequent grandchild Luke many years later.

JR would be super excited and thankful he said the choice of birthday proved he was right, she was ours not the Africans child.

When the telegram arrives at home in Georgetown announcing JR and Beatrice's first grandchild an impromptu street party was held. This was the start of a lifelong deep love for one another.

Lynette and Olawuyi were to have the shortest of marriages, Lynette had bought everything for the new baby, a cot, baby carriage nappies and was expected to do everything regarding her care. Olawuyi was not keen on the colour of the child and felt a boy child was more in his status so that did not go down well. On Christmas day just 10 days after my birth and 3 days at home a fully feathered just killed dead turkey and all Christmas provisions were laid out on the kitchen table for Lynette to prepare for the 8 guests Olawuyi had invited...It was prepared and served by only by Lynette. Needless to say, they argued and Lynette realised the distance between them would become ever greater. He was arrogant, uncaring and condescending towards her and it was up to her to decide for the future. He had the temerity to complain about her cooking and he suggested that she could satisfy his friend sexually when she refused he hit her with the back of his hand...it was to be the first and last time he would ever do that to my mother .Quick as a flash she picked up a chair and whacked him solidly on the head he fell immediately his prosthetic leg giving him no resistance. He cowered in the corner his friends attending to him and leaving directly.

Lynette had her strength back and was again invincible. The Animal's pop song " I gotta get out of this place if it's the last thing I ever do !" was playing on the radio and it was the mood music she needed.

She was to get a job as a night sister at the local hospital starting in February 1965 and so it was that the two of us went every night together to work me in my carry cot with a spare nappy and some milk. I must admit I found the work remarkably easy !

Lynette got her money together and packed her grip and my things and we left in a taxi never to return. The next time Ruthy saw Mr Babalola she was 36. She always knew she was lucky ! Meeting him in his Battersea bedsit confirmed it. Many Caribbean girls who married Africans and innocently gave the fathers their children to take to show Grandparents in the home country found the children were never returned. The child would simply disappear, or the documentation would be tampered with and thus become invalid, another person would take the passport and identity or they would just die form a tropical disease and be buried, a certificate would be given as explanation to the mother. One of Lynette's lifelong friends lost a twin child in this manner and the sole surviving twin cannot return to England as his father sold the child's passport and thus birth right. Another had her child sent away and again never saw him again. In the rare cases when a child was left with father they would drop the child with the Dr Barnardo's charity and let them be cared for by the state or the charity. Lynette subsequently divorced him and moved onwards and upward her career path to break the glass ceiling.

John Augustus Richards was as good as his word and the iconic picture which is on the cover of the book is of a small version of a 2-year-old mini me in the living room of 47 Palm Street the day before my Mother returned to England leaving me in the safest place on the planet with the greatest Grandparents ever for the next few years.

Some of the best years of my life.

So, Christine-Althea (Ruthy) is ever grateful and thankful and counts blessing which are incalculable.

VINCENT AND OWEN RICHARDS

Grandad John Richards was an ardent art lover and he particularly enjoyed the Dutch masters and Vincent Van Gogh. His favourite flower was the Helianthus annuus the Sun flower and so when his last son was born he was able to choose a name reflecting Sunshine in his older years ... as this was his last child with Beatrice the love of his life. A faithful beautiful and wise lady who he loved deeply. Little Vincent was named after Van Gogh. Vince as he was called was a tall lanky smart guy who could turn his hand to anything. He learnt fast, could fix locks, make clocks and make women cry ...Vincent was a handsome and popular guy... JR decided his energies should be channelled into study so when the 2-year-old granddaughter came to stay it was a perfect chance to arrange that Vincent go to England to study Electrical engineering at Croydon Technical College. He had already paid for the basic studies at the Georgetown Technical Institute and he was ready to expand. Vincent's ticket was delivered and yet another child would have the same farewell as all the others had enjoyed, though now it was more muted and it was so commonplace and Palm Street had changed too with many having migrated to America and Canada too.

Vincent like his sister before excelled and prospered. He had several positions along the way each time climbing up the ladder closer to becoming a Manager. First was the brick factory in Croydon, then the Bakery Mother Pride where he was Head of Production ensuring the public got their sliced bread and hot cross buns…then AI Group and right now he is head of all the Electrical and Buildings for the Department of Transport in England. He has been married along the way and has 2 Children Mathew and Michelle and 4 grandchildren He is now married to the lovely Alicia who is from Guyana. Always the fun guy and full of jokes a reliable brother. He is the only vegetarian in the family having made friends with a pet chicken only to discover his new feathery friend had become dinner he resolved never to eat meat again since age 6 and he never has.

JR would be proud of his youngest sons achievements.

Owen a real gentleman was always quiet and just being 2 years younger than fellow Libran, Lynette they were super close. Lynette sent for him and he too studied at Croydon Technical College studying Electrical engineering and specialising in environmental Health. He was ahead of his time. He had a red Volkswagen beetle which I enjoyed standing on the side bars. He was such a lovely man. He married Victoria, Vicky and she was also Guyanese and could sew too so he could see similarity with his Mother. They awaited their first born and were warned to stay well away from anyone who had rubella…on Adrian's arrival it was clear not all was well and he was unfortunate to be victim of in vitro Rubella. He would be profoundly deaf and later would also become blind but he is highly intelligent and can communicate. He lives in an adapted care home in Plymouth, Devon the city where the whole story began and enjoys gardening and community activities.

Owen looked after his little family and gained promotion in his job, they did their best to stimulate Adrian and worked ceaselessly with him a patient and loving parents. Lynette was in Guyana on a visit looking after her father JR who had become ill with his foot probably the effects of undiagnosed diabetes and got a phone call at the family home

47 Palm Street which now had a telephone...It rang and was his wife Vicky calling to say Owen was in the Royal Marsden Hospital in Surrey and Leukaemia had been diagnosed. He was already in an Isolation Unit and untouchable for hugs and warmth.

Lynette travelled home knowing she had done all she could for her beloved Father but that may well be the last embrace she would have from him. In Trinidad the plane was delayed so the passengers were put into a coastal hotel...she walked on the beach and collected the most exquisite black sea coral fern to bring home as a souvenir. It was like a stiff black lace veil. A portend of what was to come. Seeing Vicky they hugged each other on meeting at the hospital. He was in a plastic tent could not be embraced and the chemotherapy had robbed him of all is hair and much of his stature. The Royal Marsden Hospital was the place as they offered top cancer treatment care in the region did all they could but to no avail within 6 weeks her little brother whom she held in her arms on his first day of arrival at 47 Palm Street had gone home.

Beatrice could not comprehend how her child Owen had moved to such a sophisticated country and still the medical experts would not be able to save him. It was heart breaking he was just 39 and son Adrian 3.

JR had decided to call time 6 weeks earlier in November and on the last day of the year the day before 1981 would arrive hopeful and fresh and void of any blemish his beloved son Owen joined him. In a few sad weeks two stalwart members of the Richards family had died.

Both would have magnificent funerals: Owen's was standing room only with his brother and brothers in law carrying him to his last resting place. He was praised and eulogised by all his friends and colleagues he was such a kind and popular man always thinking of others. Even in all that pain he found time to tell me to study hard for my O'levels and to do my best at school ...We requested a couple of songs from the hospital radio to play a fighting song Stevie Wonder's "I ain't gonna stand for this!" against the vile cancer and " I just called to say I Love you.". He had so many blood transfusions but it was just too little, too late... it was his time .We still miss him. Aunty Vicky went on to care for Adrian and he is happy and excels. Also to remarry after 5 years widowhood to Malcom Brown and have two sons and is a grandmother, very much valued member of the family.

UNCLE OWEN AND FRIENDS AND FAMILY OUTSIDE 47 PALM STREET

Uncle Owen Richards in his hat with uncle Cyril Johdan Beryl's husband the first gentleman on the left with friends outside 47 Palm Street, Werk-en-Rust , Georgetown, British Guiana, South America. All the men in this photograph would leave British Guiana to work and study overseas, none would return.

After Lynette Left Owen, Beatrice and Vincent, JR were left .

UNCLE OWEN

Uncle Owen, me and Mummy in Redhill Surrey. Spring 1965

Owen Richards circa 1965

UNCLE VINCENT

©Vincent Richards
Vincent Richards aged 2

© Vincent Richards
Vincent Richards the gentleman aged 13 in his first pair of long trousers.

© Vincent Richards
Age 21 in London.

1966 INDEPENDENCE DAY:

GUYANA IS BORN.

On Thursday the 26th on May 1966 British Rule ceased ending 163 years of history and partnership. It was in 1814 that the British won the land from the Dutch and so British Guiana became under the British flag. The land mass was in total 214,969 sq.km about the same size as England. The population comprised of the imported people the British brought over such the African slaves at first from other islands under their control such as Barbados and later after slavery was abolished the British transferred Indian Indentured labourers from the Indian Sub-continent. The Chinese also came and built the railway and did business such as setting up small manufacturing plants and stores. Six Nationalities would ultimately make up this country . Original owners the Amerindian natives, Black Africans , English, Indian, Chinese and Portuguese.

A celebration party was organised for the county and the Act of Parliament which created The Guyana Independence Act of 1966 was enacted in Westminster. No war of independence was needed like the Americas a simple treaty and generous supportive settlement system was put in place.

The former citizens of British Guiana would have the right to remain British citizens as they were born before 1966 and the transition to independence.

It was a wonderful gift 214,969 square Kilometres of prime land … Gratis, Free!

As Mark Twain said "Buy Land, they don't make it anymore."

It had been a short time coming the years of the 1950's and early 1960's had seen a sharp economic decline with much unemployment and poverty increased and along with-it crime. Many started to survive only by the remittances sent from loved ones abroad. There were rumblings even riots and the population started to demand change and self-rule and the British listening to the colonies wishes planned to enable this desire to become reality.

The GAWU Guiana Agricultural Workers Union went on General strike for better conditions and wages bringing the country to a standstill, and on 25th July 1964 189 people were killed and 15000 workers were displaced at another riot 38 African workers were killed following a bomb explosion, this along with ethnic riots earlier in February 1962 which had led the British to send in the troops to quell the situation meant they felt that to acquiesce to the demands was the smart thing to do. They would choose the brightest and the best to become the future leaders of the former colonies giving them the chance to study law in England at the LSE London School of Economics and the Middle Temple for the bar, then return home to be the new generation of benevolent leaders for the people.

After WWII in the 1950's Guiana became unstable. Britain desperately weakened by the human cost of the war not to mention the infrastructure, demoralisation and economic woes Now Britain had to cope with the loss of territories as places seeing a chance grabbed freedom, so it was that India along with other parts of the Eastern Empire become free. The new cold war was just starting with the iron curtain and USSR a former ally in WWII turning away making its own communistic plans for their region of the world. Central Europe was defined by Capitalism and freedom in the West or Communism and repression in the East. Now the Caribbean territories begun to itch too. The British army was stretched to its limits so countries thought now was the time to play games as they could get away with any nonsense... They were wrong. It was a case of till here and no further... the British Acted. Having been generous and given the people suffrage and a free vote to have a trial run at governing themselves the PPP Peoples Progressive Party lead by charismatic dentist Dr Cheddi Jagan along with wife Janet had won the vote...He started to immediately implement laws showing his enormous disdain for the British way of life and attempted to bring direct socialism reform which was seen as a missile aimed towards the colonial powers and an entrance for Marxism on the continent. The government existed 133 days then early one morning.

Radio Berbice usual announcer was replaced by the Governor General Sir Alfred Savage.

He announced in his clipped English accent " This moment the Navy and Army are here in sufficient force to cope with any emergency that may arise and the forces are widely distributed throughout the country." This was the first that most Guianese knew about the British troops arriving and the ensuing interregnum. The British meant business. The Scottish Guards the Argyll and Southern Highlanders came and did their work ...however when they left they took the girls of Guiana to bonny Scotland with them. The girls came from well-off middle-class Guianese homes they were to live in the coldest part of Britain, Glasgow and the notorious tenement blocks as the soldiers came from poorer backgrounds using the army as a career path to a better life, it was quite a stark adjustment for the Guianese girls and some returned.

In preparation for self-rule all the accoutrements of statehood were prepared.

Guyana was the new name chosen by the majority of the citizens in a vote, the spelling change of vowel from I to Y supposedly modernising it. A new coat of arms was created with the Canje Pheasant (Opisthosomas Hoazh) chosen as the National bird the Royal Crown was replaced with the Amerindian Caciques Crown of Feathers, Two Fierce Jaguars one with a pick axe in its paw and the other with a stalk of rice and sprouting sugar cane plant the Jaguars stood either side of the shield, two brilliant diamonds represented the mining industry. A Victoria Lily which is found naturally floating gracefully on the canals of the cities and villages became the national flower. A motto chosen it was declared on the banner " One People, One Nation, One Destiny." Three wavy lines in sky blue were placed on the shield representing the three main rivers of Guyana, The Demerara River, Essequibo river, and the Berbice river.

The British Guiana National anthem of "God Save the Queen" was replaced with a new National Anthem which was penned "Dear Land of Guyana" was written by Rev Archibald Lukey with music composed by the famous musician Cyril G Potter.

And a new flag to replace the British Guiana Standard with the clipper ship emblem was created. Returning to the Amerindian roots the arrow head was selected. Designed with clean lines colours symbolising the values and wealth of the new country. The golden arrowhead was conceived by the American Whitney Smith and it was chosen to show Guyana's journey into the future.

Golden Yellow showed the tremendous mineral wealth, red the nation's zeal, black border, the peoples enduring journey to the future, the green colour represented the agricultural potential and the white the water potential.

The country had tremendous prospects and had the ability to feed itself and the rest of the Caribbean. The rich fertile strip of land provided all the provisions the nation needed, then the interior savannahs provided perfect grazing for cattle and everyone had a kitchen garden.

Guyana had an excellent railway service initiated by Cecil Rhodes and funded by the British using steam locomotives which covered

Georgetown and the coastal route this could have easily been extended to provide more expansive service throughout the land ,opening up the interior and enabling people to commute from the North to the South.

Potable Water always an issue had in many parts been solved by the British Civil engineering projects laying a series of pipelines throughout the city and towns. In the villages the local stand pipe was more usual but this too by 1966 was improving and most had internal plumbing and the water was safe to drink.

The city of Georgetown was known as the Garden City and the Botanical Gardens, Promenade and streets were decorated with lovely trees of every sort and numerous flowers were on display.

Housing was neat and simple most lived in wooden small huts on stilts due to the danger of flooding the danger were termites wood ants and sea water coming to visit after breaching the sea wall. Most had decent homes no one was on the street.

Mineral's Gold, Diamonds, Oil (undiscovered),Bauxite, good fertile agricultural land and the wonderful citizens were the greatest assets of the land. So, in 1966 the land was safe, food was plentiful, there was excellent affordable transport whether the train, boat, car or bus everything was there. Add to this an incorruptible police service, a well-trained defence force, decent clapboard homes, cultural activities , good schools and even a new university in Georgetown under the chancellorship of HM Princess Alice. The new Guyana had all that was required to build on the firm solid foundation the British were to leave for them . More than this the civil service and all government was provided too al buildings were given freely along with continued promise of support from the former colonial rulers via finance, partnership , friendship and advise. All done at a stroke of a pen. Even the Venezuelan issue where they wanted all the landmass to the West of the Essequibo river was resolved with the British support at the UN the territory was declared in law British Guiana and thus Guyana ownership.

The Event warranted a state visit the Act was duly passed and their

Royal Highness Duke and Duchess of Kent sailed forth and read HRH HM the Queen's speech to the population and Forbes Burnham duly became the new and first PM of Guyana. Every Blessing was given to the land and the people and the hand of friendship and encouragement was ever extended for Britain they were to become the 23rd country to join the best club on the planet the Commonwealth and with that enjoy superior privileges and access to England.

HRH HM the Queen and HRH Prince Philip also visited the realm and to be sure JR and Beatrice went to view and wave to their monarch. Wearing their best outfits, they cheerfully observed everything and JR was delighted to see HM in living colour after so many years on watching his Queen's portrait on the office wall. She was so beautiful and spoke so eloquently. He was to treasure that day always.

With such tremendous potential and hope what could go wrong ….Guyana surely would become another prosperous country like a Singapore or America …Let's see…Grandad JR always said " Guiana can be a paradise, we have everything gold, water, land ,great people we will be rich one day, you wait and see."

The British Troops arrival in British Guiana in 1953

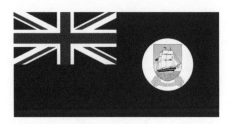

The British Guiana Flag

THE NEW COAT OF ARMS FOR THE NEW GUYANA.

Independent Guyana's Coat of Arms . 1966

THE NEW FLAG

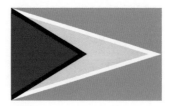

The Golden Arrowhead Flag. 1966

The Land of Guyana.

LINDON FORBES BURNHAM
VERSUS CHEDDI BERRET JAGAN

*W*hat does it take for a potentially magnificent country to be ruined ?

Ego, selfishness and vanity .

In the Bible the story of the wisdom of King Solomon there is the story about the mothers who both had a baby at the same time, only one of the children had died and there was a dispute as to who the mother of the live baby was… He held a sword above the child and did as though he would cut the living child in half thus give each mother half a child. One mother said "Yes go ahead cut him that way we both have half ." the other said " No spare the child let her have him ,let him live ."

That was the test that King Solomon used to see who was the real mother… The lady who wanted the child to live even if it went to the other woman was the real mother. How much more must you be unselfish when loving and governing a country?

Forbes Burnham and Cheddi Jagan had many commonalities, both wanted independence for Guiana, both were to attend the most elite school in the country Queen's college and both wanted to rule they were also firm friends.

Forbes was of African descent with slave ancestry and was born in a poor part of Georgetown Kitty he was to win a scholarship and become the best student in the colony earning him a free tuition scholarship place at the LSE, London School of Economics where he would study Law and become a barrister and QC. Forbes returned to British Guiana in 1949.

Dr Cheddi Jagan a son of Hindu Indians whose parents were indentured labourers from India. He attended Queens college also and from there with his father's savings went to USA where he paid his own way through medical school eventually returning to Georgetown age 25 to set up his practice and as a dentist in 1943.

They came together in a collaborative formation christened the PPP Peoples Progress Party, however due to egoism of the 2 somewhat self-absorbed charismatic characters could no longer co-exist in the same party and in the separation the Black African Party of the PNC was formed by Forbes the letters signified the Peoples National Council.

Though they both agreed that self-rule and determination was needed despite the generosity and largesse of the colonial power they wanted to feel how it was to be free to make their own destiny and dreams for statehood evolved and for the society they would create for the peoples. The citizens had no great complaints as they did in South Africa or Southern states of USA ,they lived in relative security and life was pretty good. Law and order were excellent with the streets being safe, the policemen walked their beats only with a baton ,no guns and they were approachable, trustworthy and incorruptible.

Violence between races was rare. Racial and religious discrimination was not tolerated, every family had every creed and colour within it so equity thrived via intermarriage. People of British Guiana would visit each other's place of worship and celebrate all manner of holy days Hindu, Christian and other beliefs so culturally everyone was aware of the different customs, traditions and understood that basically they were all the same and one nation.

Educationally there was a massive disconnect between those who lived in the city and the countryside. Only the elite and highly intelligent would make the grade to attend high school in the capital city, Queens College being number one then Tutorial High School second, this was where Lynette won her scholarship to attend. These schools enabled the students to study English exams at O' and A' level GCSE's.

Never mind they would have to write an essay with the subjects being "A day on the streets of London" or describe "a snowy day." When they had never seen it. Still they did their best work and passed with excellent grades. However, in the countryside the need for educated farm and sugar workers was never a reality so the rural areas school was finished for the people at 13 after getting the basics of literacy so they could work on the land. They would be literate enough to read a local newspaper and bible but not more lest they learnt too much and became discontent with their lot in life. For the most part these folks did not own land or property and had contentment with the simplicity of their lives planting rice paddy and cutting sugar cane. Church on Sunday and pleasant days.

In Georgetown most lived in a yard in a lot system and in clapboard homes only the very wealthy lived in spacious palaces in Bel Air but the homes were decent, clean and welcoming. Georgetown was also the place to be seen either in the markets of Bourda and Stabroek or big market, here we have Regent street, Bookers Department store and the Carnegie Library where literature could be borrowed freely. It was the place to be seen and the place to be.

The British encouraged enterprise and business thrived with innovativeness being rewarded with the establishment of various commercial enterprises which added to the economy.

While there were several newspapers and radio stations they were censored so as not to stir up any resentment towards the colonial authorities. The economy was stable with £1 equal to $5 local dollars today £1 is equal to $500 local currency.

With the former slave's children and indentured labourer's offspring travelling abroad and studying seeing new lifestyles and becoming exposed to new ideologies they would become dissatisfied with their lot in life in Guiana and hence the formation of the PPP and subsequently the PNC. Cheddi had married Janet an American Jewish lady with a strong socialist conviction. Forbes said he believed the same but deep inside was actually far more left wing than anyone knew. His true dream was to create in Guiana a Communist Marxist state but he kept this to himself eluding to the British and Americans that he was the one they needed to back to save South America from Communism that the Moderatism style Socialism Cheddi PPP wanted to implement for the good of all the people.

Both would protest to the colonial powers that too much income from the colony was being diverted to the Mother Country and that Guiana was in dire need of infrastructure projects such as bridges, ports, housing , education especially in rural communities and better health care facilities countrywide. They insisted they were up for the task if only they were given the chance to rule themselves.

Forbes Burnham played the race card from the bottom of the deck and Cheddi followed suit. This politicised the volatile situation by stirring up hatred that was never there before, stating that the PNC was for the Black Africans and the country as a whole belonged more to them as they had been there the longest apart from the Amerindians. The PPP did likewise and even today this still resonates. Forbes joined up with the innocent Peter D'Aguilar the Rum magnate who had the conservative leaning Unionist Party and was tricked by Burnham to join in collation, Peter later realised he was tricked subsequently withdrew from politics and became a .strong force against the PNC. The PPP who naturally had all the Indian majority votes and would therefore win with their political rhetoric and message. With universal suffrage in 1953 Cheddi won honestly but the troops were called and the next time proportional representation was used to count the votes and the PNC won! The first President was Arthur Chung Chinese gentleman and British trained Lawyer and Judge he was well liked by the locals but would be ousted from power.

Forbes Burnham became the Prime Minister of the newly independent Guiana he accompanied HRH HM the Queen Elizabeth II on her 1966 visit and admired the crowds who came out to welcome her. This was to be the start of 28 years of misery and hardship as all imports were banned. Self-sufficiency was the law enforced for the majority of the citizens. If Guyana could not produce a product it was not available in the shops …Guyana did not produce cotton, wheat flour, paraffin used for cooking stoves and as the population would find out much more. The privileged elite still were able to get anything they wanted so Forbes did not suffer.

Like a frog in a pan of water on the fire, only when the temperature was so high and the water was boiling did the populous realise they were with the wrong side and had been duped.

Many Guyanese Born British Citizens emigrated citizens in GB enthusiastically embraced the ideals of their new nation. Burnham would visit London and recruit them with his promises and pull on their patriotism to return to help build up the country. One such gentleman was Mr St Elmo Hughes already a highly distinguished teacher in GB. He was blissfully married to the beautiful Doreen and they had two children Laurie and Lorraine. Both worked and he was an expert teacher in demand. St Elmo had been head hunted by the prestigious Harrison College the top Elite school in Barbados and was attending a farewell party where Burnham was also at the new Guyana High Commission in Notting Hill. Burnham reprimanded him stating he should not go to Bridgetown and Harrison but return instead to his roots and Guyana. Forbes argument and promises of a house, salary and benefits was so persuasive that he declined the offer and instead flew over Barbados to Guyana and set up the new Education Ministry and implemented best Tuition practice for his countrymen. All went well in the beginning but after the glorious welcome there were stirrings of dissent and like the child catcher in chitty chitty bang bang the happy colours of the wagon fell off revealing the evil side of life. Murder bloodshed, disappearances, mystery illnesses and leaders like Walter Rodney dared to speak and form opposition and talk of Pan Africanism, withdrawal for GB commonwealth and removal of Forbes…Burnham became jealous, paranoid thinking rightly that everyone was against him. Walter Rodney had set up a very popular political party which would challenge him and could have won …had it not been for his untimely death in a most egregious manner. He was walking along las usual listening to his transistor radio close to his ear when it blew up taking his life and the hopes of many with him. It was called a malfunction! St Elmo knew he was no longer flavour of the month along with many others who had come he came to realise Forbes was a liar and master manipulator. It was clear he was on the list to be eliminated... it was just a matter of time. Many of his friends and colleagues had disappeared or tried to flee only to be imprisoned or worse in the process. No one was paid salary, electricity was as rare as hens teeth, food was expensive and scarce and there was danger everywhere. Guyana was a dreadful sad place the paradise had gone. To save his family and their future he planned his escape. Elmo would leave his wider family and parents in-laws behind and would never return to Guyana. He left as if it was another ordinary day going with his briefcase to school nonchalantly greeting the neighbours and townsfolk sharing a little humour and a loving smile as he walked along. Only today he was leaving forever, his heart in his throat tearful red eyes absorbing all he could photographing in his minds eye the country he loved. He got to the "safe" awaiting taxi his family had secured for him and drove to Timehri airport one way ticket in another name and passport, to catch the BOAC plane to London and freedom of sorts. He had sent his family on ahead on a so called vacation and they were all reunited in London. Heartbroken but not down and out they recovered financially because of the solidarity of the family and great love they shared, career wise he went on to become the first black headmaster in London for the Tulse Hill School in Lambeth commuting 3 hours a day from his family home in Leytonstone. His wife Doreen became top directors company secretary with Royal Dutch Shell. Lorraine followed in her fathers footsteps and is a top educationalist and Laurie is a brilliant business man building hospitals all over the world and making computer systems. Elmo is remembered and missed by all who were lucky to know him and he made a massive impact on thousands of children's lives through his happy countenance and amazing teaching methods. Had he been able to stay and succeed who knows what wonders he could have done with the children of Guyana. It was a great loss and he was one of the thousands of super talented patriots who left their good homes in GB to help only to be disappointed and fortunate to be one of the lucky ones who survived to have such stories to tell. They left and from their airline window looked out over the land knowing they had chosen the right path… Burnham continued his dystopian, tragic, cruel, corrupt governing style and was determined to stay in power at any cost.

Elections were rigged several times and the British TV programme confronted him with the facts that the 67,000 overseas voters were fictitious he continued with the charade even physical evidence found such as discarded ballot papers which were pro PPP floating in the Demerara River did admit potential fraud but still he stayed.

Forbes Burnham changed the constitution in 1980 removing the Presidential role as a figurehead but placing it with executive monarchical powers. He changed the name now also to The Cooperative Republic of Guyana. This election needed a 2/3rds majority amazingly he would take an unprecedented 97% of the vote and win without opposition. Now with the stolen mandate he continued inflicting damage and despair on his people. His original supporters had long since departed but he continued to act as though they regarded him as a hero in his grasp. He changed the name again to be The Cooperative Republic of Guyana and eroded links to England further by renouncing Guyanese ability to receive titles in recognition of good works from HM Queen Elizabeth II Honours List, now Guyana would make its own medals and awards and hand them out internally, the Arrow head awards era was here.

As a mayor of Georgetown in the early 1960's he would roam around the city on his horse and look down on the city folk, a sport he would continue to do throughout his political career. The black African' divide in terms of employment was such that the black African supporters would be in the army, police force and civil service with Indian's on the land or business. The racial divide was stark and continues to resonate even today.

But the worst that Burnham had a duplicitous nature, in his

political career he pretended that he was a reasonable socialist when all the while he had disastrous plans for the poor down trodden citizens. The plan was unveiled it was called inspirationally "Feed, Clothe and House the Nation Plan." Unveiled in 1973 by Dr Kenneth King Minister of Economic Development. Under this plan Guyana was to be moulded into a great society which was completely self-reliant eventually to become and egalitarian under cooperative socialism. They were only economic with the truth of the 65,000 homes that were to be built only 5000 were built. Excuses included shortage of cement, wood flood and rain etc. Realty was that he was not getting the income he expected from the sugar, bauxite and rice.

As for clothing the plan was to grow and only wear home grown cotton ...the Chinese provided a cotton textile factory in Ruimvelt region of Georgetown and the cotton which was cultivated by members in the national service not willing farmers and was poor not only in quality but quantity and cotton had to be imported form USA . defeating the object of being super independent so fabric continued to be imported and due to the economic woes at home the populations GDP fell so low they could not afford clothing and it became a make do a mend as there was a virtual wage freeze and inflation.

Where people may have been poor and unable to afford clothes or luxuries for the home never had they encountered hunger there was always excess. For the first-time malnutrition opened its skeletal outstretched arms to welcome Guyana to the hungry and famine club. Guyana had always been an agricultural using the rich coastal strip to plant food and people always had a kitchen garden with a few chickens and vegetables. Most had a fruit tree in the yard and so most could survive hard times...but when the cupboards are bare and the fields yield nothing ...starvation is close by .It started with disastrous politicised racially motivated agricultural policies. Rice a staple was curtailed ,first no more rice was sold to Cuba so no income, then Connell Rice and Sugar company were drafted to regulate the surplus rice on the world market...this led to a total loss of income of $7 million losses to the Rice Marketing Board and thus the economy. In addition, the PNC withdrew concessions like duty free gasoline for agricultural vehicles, cheap fertilizers. Then the body blow all rice had to be sold at an incredibly low price to the government who would then resell at a higher price keeping the profit for themselves. Rice production naturally declined leading to shortages steering regular customers like Jamaica and Trinidad to look elsewhere for supplies.

Milk production and sugar cane suffered similar fates.

Water protection including drainage canals and irrigation was forgotten for prestige projects like the longest pontoon bridge across the Demerara River and unproductive infrastructure with narrow roads but employing many PNC supporters the Afro-Guyanese.

1976 was the year projected when Guyana would feed and clothe itself was the year that people starved and those that had family outside would be grateful for foreign currency or a food packet that arrived with provisions. Lynette would send her parents a food packet each week and all Palm street would benefit. Children in families who had no one abroad suffered and the mental impact of lack of nutrition exists even to this day in the capacity to learn and grow. Elderly died and more who could leave the country did so never to return. Many unwitting enthusiastic expats from the UK and USA who were settled in these new countries had heeded to call and sweet words of Forbes Burnham to return from abroad to rebuild the country, but when they came suitcases in hand and high hopes they found food lines, and a dictator who was dangerously arrogant and unaware of the failing reality of his vision. Many would flee back to the certainty of life in England and the places where they had gone to before, no one stayed. Lynette too had considered returning to share her knowledge with the new Guyana but JR and Beatrice said "No stay where you are in England, it's no longer safe."

Worse would come Trains, Flour and Jonestown! It would seem that when Forbes dream was being disrespected by the people he became more envious and exceedingly bitter toward the old colonial country of England. This would not bode well for the citizens. He was heavily into black power and pan Africanism and was vindictive. Having studied with many current African leaders at the LSE such as

Sir Seretse Khama of Botswana, Kwame Nkrumah of Ghana and Erol Barrow Barbados he wanted to compete with them and let his Guyana shine but because he had made such a mess of the economy there was Stagflation where the wheel barrow was worth more than the money inside ...They printed money .Hard currency was scarce so they sold the family silver. Faked wheat flour instead using rice flour and telling the people it was their fault when the bakes and roti did not work as per the recipes. Crime and hunger became common.

In the early days of his rule Lynette had sent her daughter to stay with her parents at first as with the frog analogy all was normal I attended Miss Cox kindergarten school and would have a packed lunch and slate and chalk to take to school. Life was still idyllic in the late 1960's- early 1970's Granny and I would often pop to see Aunt Pauline in BV and we always travelled in the train 2nd class and I would have the window seat a nice wooden slatted chair and would enjoy surveying the coastal scenes, it was always a cheerful atmosphere with everyone sharing fudge and coconut water. This time though the impression was sombre with people crying even granny was looking outside with me not chatting as usual .Naturally I asked why and then another lady came with her grandchild and the already full train was full to bursting and I had to sit on Granny's lap. Granny Beatrice said "This is last train Burnham is selling them." No wonder everyone was miserable they understood the tremendous impact it would have on their lives and their futures. Forbes Burnham sold the trains lock stock and barrel. The frog was now in hot water... No mind the positive energy, safety and advancement that they had brought to the vast country. Cecil Rhodes had even visited and advised the building of this amazing project. Every Race had participated in the building of the railway, Chinese came especially from China to help, Black Africans, Indians everyone worked and was impacted positively by these Cheerful Steam engines. But Mr Burnham had run out of money and needed desperately foreign currency so they sold the jewel in the crown to pay for day to day needs .The country has never recovered and numerous people have died in car crashes and road traffic accidents, more have lost limbs it is a fact that when you have good mass transport fewer accidents occur as they are usually safer than everyone going on the roads. There are numerous victims and those that unfortunately loose limbs cannot easily access a prosthetic limb so are doomed to beg. The country went from being a forward moving country which could have extended the railway to one which was back to where it was in 1848. The Demerara Berbice Railway had two railway line the Georgetown to Berbice line closed in 1972 .

Now the Black and Indian Population ate rice as a staple but also each day Indians would have a roti with their meal. By banning the importation of Wheat flour and insisting they use inferior home-grown rice flour he basically starved the Indian population such a thing would not be forgiven or forgotten, it led to more racial tension. So much so that if as visitor you came home to get a taxi and were not the same race as the taxi chauffer he would refuse to carry you, same in shops for service, health care and such like. Guyana went backwards swiftly. So, more people left as the country had crippled itself by removing its backbone railways and had embraced racial discord.

At the same time the great and the good came to Guyana President Josef Tito of Yugoslavia leader of the Non-Aliened Movement, J. Nehru of India , J. Nyere of Tanzania and Kwame Nkrunah of Ghana came to meet in Georgetown and see the progress of the Marxist experiment and praise their comrade as a great man.

Later inhabitants in the city were banned from keeping chickens saying it was not modern or hygienic but this meant all the chickens and livestock had to be slaughtered meat became scarce and a luxury for those in the city. JR lost his chickens too.

Post was anticipated not only by the recipient but also by the post office. The corruption meant that any card or letter that had a smidgeon of bulk would be intercepted and the valuable currency removed before arrival. The citizens suffered tremendously. The Black African population had already earlier chosen not to support Burnham but he rigged the elections so even when they did not vote for him he still "won" so the evil situation continued and the usual answer to "How are you ?" became " I am trying ." basically trying to survive.

Lynette sent food packages filled with packets of Vesta meals which were dry and just needed water to be added, Complan in all flavours was also popular especially the chicken soup, tinned sardines and Frey bentos meat pies in the tin and some chocolate.

At one point an egg per 8 days was the permitted ration and if one could be found it was $1000 hyperinflation dollars. Lines were everywhere based on a rumour that someone had cooking oil, paraffin, eggs or meat. It could have been the USSR . Pensions were worthless. The young and the elderly suffered most the youth just left so the brain drain continued with people leaving to G.B ,USA and Canada.

Mr Jim Jones was a charismatic Marxist minded preacher who supposedly wanted a "home land" that was safe for his flock. Forbes Burnham invited him to Guyana and settle there. He chose to offer the Preacher man a location called St Mathews ridge close to the Venezuelan border to build Jonestown. The Peoples Agricultural Temple This was the North West aspect of Guyana and Jim Jones paid cash in US $ so hard currency. There were 3 main reasons he permitted them to set up home there the first was the money 2nd it was felt that the Venezuelans would not invade Guyana as long as it was populated 3rd American citizens would be protected by America so Venezuela would not antagonise them. All was going swimmingly but Jim Jones was a psychopathic man with an ego the size of a small country and his paradise namesake was a hell on earth for those who had left their comfortable homes in San Francisco to build the dream soon became a dystopian reality and not the agricultural utopia they had naively hoped for. Over 900 souls were to drink the cyanide laced Kool aid and die in the jungle. Congressman Leo Ryan who had come to check up on his constituents and some of his media crew were first to be attacked . This was on 18th November 1978.

Forbes Burnham's legacy depends on how you view history. For the many he was a dictator, short sighted and cruel, stirring up racial tension where there was none, destroying the legacy and rebutting the gifts left by the British and others for his own ends. He freely gave Guyanese citizens who were qualified as doctors, nurses, teacher and engineers to help other African countries develop and grow . More than this he insisted that intellectuals also did manual labour on the fields ...those who had believed in his promises came back from overseas to help build the land only to run away when they faced the awful reality that it was a Marxist experiment of a megalomaniac. They ran for their lives back to the security and peace of USA and England never to return to their homeland until he died. When Guyana was in dire straits not one of these African countries returned the favour, not even one solitary nurse was sent. Botswana still has the legacy of the Guyanese teachers who went for a short sojourn to assist ...they never returned and the education service in Guyana has not recovered.

On infrastructure the positive is the pontoon bridge crossing the Demerara River ,his ideals of nationalism and self-sufficiency while good should have been done in a spirit of continued friendship with England and not in a Marxist manner. His desire for power kept him in power for 28 years during which many died due to malnutrition, people suffered long power outages and more citizens left never to return . He knew he was not liked and when he needed surgery to remove a bone in his throat, they say that he died for want of the instrument to remove the blockage it could not be found... He was embalmed for posterity. Few mourned him.

Cheddi Jagan finally after waiting for 28 years would become the 4th President of Guyana. His Prime Minister was of Black African descent Sam Hinds. He was not bitter in spite of having won so many elections and having the mandate stolen from him. For all his socialism he was a moderate and did his best to get on with all countries and Guyana missed the statesman and his good leadership because of Forbes egoistic nature so many suffered. It was never proven that he too was a Marxist but many believe he would never have driven the country down to such depths of sadness where so many sought a way out either by boat, plane of the weed killer route. Guyana had the highest rate of suicide in the world and favourite method was the drinking of poison. We pray for good leaders with vision and integrity. Many Guyanese hail him as the father of the nation. His wife became the first female president after him and inaugurated the Cheddi Jagan International Airport and the research centre. His son named for him also became a dentist also and the Dr Cheddi Jagan dental surgery is still in Georgetown.

LEADERS OF A NEW NATION

Dr Cheddi Jagan

Dr Cheddi Jagan with future Prime Minister of Israel Levi
Eshkol 1961

Forbes Burnham in Cuba with Castro

The Burnham Legacy.

JOHN AUGUSTUS RICHARDS
1900-1980

*J*ohn Richards enjoyed a leisurely retirement, he did a little gardening, played dominos and community youth work. He could take care of the chickens and the yard area. He was busy with the Freemasons lodge where he had over the years risen in the ranks of Freemasonry and they did much charitable work in the Georgetown. He was content all his children were now abroad and doing well ,he had frequent visits from them and now the grandchildren came too.

*H*e had hoped that when all their training was done the would be able to return permanently and live in Guyana but the turbulent times of Independence meant that he selflessly told them to stay in safety in England. Independence was a bitter blow for most Guyanese who felt duped with Burnham's regime and lamented quietly how he was squandering not only the wealth of the country but the strong friendly ties previously enjoyed with the West. People who protested loudly ended up as a corpse with no one witnessing how they lost their lives. These were dangerous times.

Now those who wanted to leave were not as welcome in the new countries…There was nowhere to go.

However, he continued doing his level best. Then he had recently an issue with his little toe which he had stubbed when jumping down from his hammock. He had never slept in a bed since his jungle days in Venezuela. For some reason it was not healing and now circulation was feeling strange. Already on a salt free diet he dreaded much more draconian remedy.

The Doctor said it was dying with gangrene and must be removed

.

JR balked at the idea of surgery and kept quietly suffering until the other toes began to do the same . On returning to the doctor the verdict was swift. His children sent money for the surgery as all the best hospitals and health care is private and he was taken from Georgetown hospital to the Mercy Hospital run by the Seventh Day Adventist where the offending foot was removed completely as it had become gangrenous.

A bitter blow for JR ,Vincent his youngest son came from England and went directly from the plane to the hospital and carried him home and cared for his father as his father had once cared for him.

As he left so Lynette came to nurse him though now in management far removed from deb pans and bandages, she had not forgotten her training of Somerset and she took everything with her to help her stricken beloved father including the infamous Lavender Water to refresh him and keep him feeling comfortable.

The day before she had arrived he was already at home weakened but still vital and in fighting form his stump was the cruel cut for the proud man and he was devastated and wondered how Beatrice would cope with the situation . Beatrice was so thankful that her daughter was there to assist and give support, she was getting to and age too. In the 2 weeks that Lynette stayed they were able to celebrate Christmas together, Lynette requested a wheel chair but, in the meantime, JR got to grips with the wooden crutches and managed to get around the home. The place was always busy with friends calling round and playing dominos or discussing politics .

When Lynette left in the plane she looked out of the window seeing the great broccoli of the jungle beneath and sparse lights and thought of all the potential the country had and how it had been squandered .The most valuable assets, the people had left …she felt as though her heart would break. Here she was an assistant unit general manager at one of the best equipped facilities in London , where invalidated and out-dated equipment was thrown away and that she had given so much time and energy to Great Britain's NHS and still nothing had changed in Guyana and it was only getting worse. Imagine no wheelchairs for an amputee, no medication for the pain. How would Mummy cope on her own with Daddy she wondered. The bright lights of Trinidad approached here there would be 24 hours lay over.

The great man my Grandfather John Augustus Richards died peacefully in his home 47 Palm Street with his friends and family around and Beatrice holding his hand. It was All Souls Night and he joined countless souls that November night. As John Richards lay in his coffin his son Patrick removed his wedding ring to the chagrin of Beatrice. He would join his father within 6 months. All over the place in JR's sight were pictures of the children and grandchildren. His funeral was attended by all and sundry the top people came all the Lodge came and it was one of the largest seen in Bourda. Father Goodrich officiated now a middle-aged man and the bells rang out for him. Beatrice embroidered a cream dress with purple flowers design and wore that with her hat and gloves her many friends came along with sister's Beryl and Pauline and Pansy came in from America JR's God daughter.

JR is buried at St Sidwell's churchyard Georgetown on the Eastern front and he is still remembered with kind words and immense gratitude. His favourite hymn "Eternal Father Strong to Save." was played.

May his memory be a blessing.

JOHN AUGUSTUS RICHARDS

JOHN AUGUSTUS RICHARDS
DIRECTOR OF BOURDA MARKET

John Augustus Richards the Director and Chief Market Officer of
Bourda Market at his office. Note the two telephones.

John Augustus Richards the young police constable in his uniform.

WHERE ARE THEY NOW?

The descendants of George Brown and John Richards have all found success in our lives in England, Canada and America, no one is left in Guyana. There have been heart breaking moments along the way. We learnt that the family is just like a soft fluffy dandelion flower at seed stage once the first flower seeds are blown away one can never be complete again, and so it is that the family unit once broken remains such. Whether at invitation of the Mother country England to study or making their own way for love. The unity and solidarity is never as complete or strong again.

There is always someone absent or excused. None of the weddings were attended by their parents. John Augustus Richards never left his country of Guyana but through his selfless vision and encouragement he secured a brilliant future for all his children. None of them would stay in the land all would leave the shores for work, training, school and opportunities which Guyana could not supply. As British born Citizens born before independence each of his children were able to move to the Mother Country of England.

All of Beatrice's sisters had left and although Pauline and Beryl would return they were also never able to connect all together again as in days of old. Hilda would remain in USA traversing between Washington DC and New York where her daughter Gloria had lived and her grandchildren had established themselves in their careers. After reaching the age of 75 Hilda stopped working with the Goldstein family. She had seen the children grow up become lawyers and doctors and cared for their children too…she had become part of the family and celebrated with them all their holidays. As Hector had literally stayed sat in the aptly named "La-Z-Boy "Chair the house had deteriorated around them and after it was condemned the grandchildren took Granny Hilda to NYC to live with them .She finally was given the rest she deserved and spent 3 years in vacation like bliss in the rest home…The grandchildren understood that their lives were massively improved because of Hilda's willingness to emigrate from Guyana it meant they were born in the land of thee free in America. Hilda died in NYC after staying at a nursing home paid for by her grandchildren. Hector, they left in Washington DC he died within a few weeks pining for his chair and TV. He was placed in a local old people's institution and on his demise was not missed and was mourned solely by his son George no eulogy, no flowers, no casket. A pauper's funeral, corpse laid in a cardboard coffin for the man whose slothful existence epitomised the sadness of selfishness and refusal to contribute anything back to his adopted country of 40 years.

Son George Thomas now works in administration for a Diabetes charity in Washington DC and he has never been back to Guyana. George Thomas has fought for his adopted country and was conscripted to be an officer in the US Navy during the Vietnam war, he served in a submarine and got an honorary discharge. On his return to civvy street he was honoured with medals for his bravery, he had thought he would be able to get excellent jobs after his service but unfortunately the Vietnam war was not popular and so he faced unemployment at first on his return.

Lynette is the Star, she became renown for her pioneering career and was the 1st ever Black lady to become a Unit General Manager, the highest rung of the health service. Lynette was responsible for moving and closing the old St Georges Hospital from its location in Kensington and opening the new departments in the Tooting site. While there in Kensington a box of silver buckles from graduating SRN's was being thrown away and Lynette rescued one so she finally after 40 years of service received her SRN graduation present. In her role as Unit General Manager she was responsible for the health and welfare of all the women's services in the borough…some 2 million people. The move of the old St Georges Hospital from its site in Knightsbridge to the brand-new building complex also changed the name and it was reborn St Georges University Hospital in Tooting, the South London Borough of Wandsworth. More than this Battersea is within the borough of Wandsworth her area of jurisdiction and now St Georges University Hospital is seen an excellent safe place to have a child just like Hillingdon was back in 1964.

She did her work excellently. Two thousand babies were safely delivered by her hands to their mothers

Although she did not return to Guyana to become Matron of Georgetown Hospital she has done her best for her homeland and is credited with setting up the Deaf aid charity which goes country wide testing hearing and providing hearing aids to fit the needs of the patient. The charity which she set up with a friend AGNAP.org the Association of Guyanese Nurses and Allied Professions has helped thousands of Guyanese in health care giving medical equipment and patient care material and finance. Lynette was the first President of AGNAP. They went on to enjoy the honour of having as Patron of AGNAP for over 25 years HE Mrs Singh the lovely wife of the High Commissioner of Guyana in Great Britain, His Excellency Lalashwar K.M Singh, whose was an enthusiastic and stalwart supporter of AGNAP. In turn Guyana through his recommendation recognised and honoured the tremendous achievements they as a charity had made to Guyanese Citizens of all creeds and colour in giving them the Medal of Honour.

In this way so many of the nurses who came as young ladies in their hats and gloves all those years ago have made an impact on 2 continents with their care, expertise and devotion to their homeland and their work in the new home country of England and the NHS. They raised money by having concerts, food fares, educational talks, all now ladies of certain age who all those years ago heeded the call to come and help the Mother country and they have. Indeed, there was a BBC programme made available on You tube called the 'Black Nurses the women who saved the NHS.'which features Lynette Richards-Lorde among others explaining their lives and contribution. Of courses they all reminisce about the £9:00 monthly salary, cold temperature and hard work but they made lifelong friends and worked solidly and cheerfully making their homes in England and having good livelihoods there too.

Aunty Nan (Nancy) married her childhood sweetheart Freddie Frank who came from her village in Beterverwagteng to England to work. They were childhood sweethearts. Freddie Frank's family had a smallholding and were a generous family able to share and ride out the storms of unemployment by having their own smallholding with vegetables, fruit and chickens. When he came to Oxford Nancy Paid his fare and he found work in a local factory. For a wedding present JR and Beatrice sent from Guyana all manner of clothes and bedlinen to them and they had one son my cousin Douglas a computer engineer. Now a widow Nancy Frank, worked solidly in the John Radcliffe hospital her entire career and was given a great send off when she eventually retired. She died in Oxford at 94 years of age.

Granny Beatrice Eudora Richards was the final owner of 47 Palm Street Werk-en-Rust, Georgetown. She was approaching 80 years old when her granddaughter whom she and JR had loved and cared for all those years ago and had taken her into the iconic family home and returned her charge to daughter Lynette in London, via Gatwick Airport her first time travelling on a plane aged 66. That was to be the first time she saw all her children and grandchildren together in England and she stayed 6 months. Well that same grandchild she cared for returned the favour and went to Georgetown this time laden with 2 grips which were laden with provisions, it was Burnham Marxist regime after all. On arrival at home all the suitcases were opened and the treasured food, salmon tins, sardines, complan energy drink, sweets tea, oil, coffee and much more came out all the neighbours were called and the sharing began. Palm Street was still the same everyone got something precious and that just eased the harshness of their lives .People pulled up a chair and sat on the window ledge outside listening and sharing the conversations and news.

Guyana independent in the 1970's to 1980's had become a difficult place, crime was up, water was undrinkable and the pipe network was in serious need of upgrade as there was cross contamination. It was still sunny place people smiled but the absence of all those who had migrated impacted society. Everything had declined in terms of standards of living ,education service ,healthcare and prices were astronomical for the average citizen. My task was to persuade this grand lady to do as her children had done and at 79 to come to live in England whether her time would be long or short I asked her to come to England to live with us. Aunt Pauline had also passed on now so only sisters Hilda and Beryl were left and both were abroad... It was a shocking idea to her but it made sense...

Two months later a spritely aged 79 Granny got on a flight to go away from all she knew ...She had spoken in spirit to her father George Brown, mother Queenie and Uncle Charlie in their Beterverwagteng resting place and to Grandad John Richards at his last earthly home at St Sidwell's Georgetown and had received their definite approval. Saying her good byes to all her friends at church, in her ladies' club and everyone in Palm Street and she too packed her grips and left as her children had before...Closing her front door for the last time, touching number 47 made by son Vincent with Mahalia Jackson's "Bless this House" playing in her head...feeling that indeed every word was true and 47 Palm Street, Werk-en-Rust, Georgetown had been a truly blessed house a wonderful home. She adjusted her hat and fixed it with the hat pin and entered the taxi with her waiting friends and drove away from her home of sixty years for the last time waving at her lifelong neighbours along the way.

Beatrice's precious companion which had provided for the welfare of the family and sewn garments for customers without prejudice her Singer sewing machine was to be left behind so the only thing she insisted on from Lynette was that she would get a new friend sewing machine at Lynette's home…

She arrived at London Gatwick Airport the sign on arrival said "Welcome to London." After a short drive down the M23 she entered 12 Woodland Way in Shirley her new home. Beatrice's bedroom suite which was to be her new domain, here she saw a new friend her new blue sewing Singer machine. On opening her suitcase with all her belongings, the first dress she picked out was the cream dress with the purple flowers which she had worn for Grandad's funeral. She held it up and said " When I die this is the outfit you must dress me in. I am relying on you."

It was to be worn some 16 years later !

Granny became my constant travelling companion going to Canada to see her sister Beryl and Cyril, Pat, Kevin and the other family members. We did the Maid of the Mist at Niagara Falls and then went by Greyhound to Washington DC to see the sights and of course Hilda and Hector…then New York and Gloria. We also went to Amsterdam; Portugal and she saw Germany. She won a raffle prize and got an all paid vacation to Malta and herself and Lynette went together. Granny Beatrice finally was able to attend family events and had a massive 80th Birthday Party in Shirley Croydon at Lynette home, celebrating each subsequent year and attended her grandchildren's weddings and met new grandchildren in person instead of via the photographs. She loved watching Colombo and reading romantic novels. When she too was diagnosed with a cataract she elected to use drops instead of having an operation …she was able to see clearly all her life.

When she got her old age pension, she requested it in £5:00 notes and each week she would send about 6-7 envelopes to her friends back in Guyana to help them out. Beatrice joined the local church St Georges the Martyr in Shirley and she became a very popular member with many many genuine friends one in particular was Carole who came by most weeks for afternoon tea and a chat. Lucky for us she was always sewing making clothes or embroidery which we still have. For the little premature babies at the Special Care unit in St Georges University Hospital she would design and sew small quilts to help them thrive under the protection of a blanket of love. She was so proud of the massive achievements her children had made and loved Christmas day when Lynette would take the family to do the rounds at St Georges hospital.

At 80 her golden rule of never wearing trousers was to change when she saw HRH HM the Queen wearing a pair …only then it was okay, she thought. At 96 she joined John Augustus Richards, Owen, her twin boys, Pauline, Charlie and her parents and was sent off in grand style with Horses and a carriage coach. It was a standing room only occasion. Her great grandson Jonathan read one of her eulogies and she is buried in Beckenham Cemetery London, George Brown and Queenie would have been smiling on their daughter's bravery and her incredible kindness and generosity. Jonathan would go on to have his bar mitzvah in Jerusalem and would visit Uman at Jewish New Year, and at 18 join the IDF and fight for Israel, so in the end its full circle. He is now policeman and will go on to be a D.I.

Father Goodrich retired and returned to England after 45 years to enjoy a well-earned rest in the college of St Barnabas Lingfield, Surrey he was still incredibly active and popular. He was the priest who would officiated at Granny's funeral in St Georges Church Shirley. He died age 94 on 6th September 2021 and is buried at the Garth in College of St Barnabas. He had a special motorcycle cortege in memory of how he travelled the length and breadth of Guyana and his funeral was well attended by his family and Guyanese friends. www.fatherderek.com

Though the years lifelong friendships have been made from the shared but uncommon experiences they encountered through daring to take up the challenge of leaving home and planting roots on the other side of the world and succeeding with excellence all the way.

So, what did Christine-Althea (Ruthy) do? Well she reconnected to Judaism and by right of return made Alijah a dream of most Jews and became an Israeli citizen id number 332332097 and became the first lady of colour to become an Honorary Consul joining the diplomatic corps and she was chosen by The Republic of Suriname to represent them in Israel this was the first time they would have representation on a diplomatic level. This she did for 10 years 2008-2018. She was also the first to bring a Guyanese Agriculture minister to Israel to see what can be done in terms of fishing, production and technology. Ruthy also took an Israeli team of water engineers and agronomists there to assist with Water purification for Georgetown and met the PNC leader H E President Jagdeo, he was most welcoming and very interested in working with us. On a diplomatic level she was instrumental in the Agriculture Master plan being made for Suriname, has made deals possible for telecom investments in Suriname and arrange educational programmes enabling people to come to Israel to study. Lately she was recently successful in getting the Paramaribo University Anton de Kom new accommodation, including new housing for students and an auditorium a making a positive impact on the country. She worked tirelessly for Suriname and Israel to connect on Education, Culture and in Business. Now happily married with family spends time between GB, Africa and Caribbean

Lynette still continues to do good works for Guyana and with friends and colleagues through her charity Agnap, and has done much work in Croydon and the South East area to assist women's health. She was one of the many charity workers volunteers who were able to walk behind Princess Diana's funeral cortege to mourn her passing as Princess Diana was the Patron for the Commonwealth Society for the Deaf for which Lynette was a Director raising funds for the Guyana Audiology service.

Lynette has been President of both the Inner Wheel Croydon and the Soroptimist's Croydon branch and is a Diabetes champion. Having initiated the audiology service in Guyana, Lynette went on to start the breakfast club in Beterverwagteng enabling children to have a nourishing meal every morning, many families could not afford food for their children and the school grades and growth was being stunted.

Career wise Lynette was director of Nursing and Midwifery for South London Hospital for Women and Children, the Weir Hospital and St Georges university Hospital. Responsible for all the regional Neonatal Services for the London borough of Wandsworth… Because of her pioneering work she was head hunted to be Director for Maternity Alliances and gave advice to Government Select Committees on Continuity of care and gave advice at the EU in Strasbourg on the same. Lynette was also selected by the NHS to represent the UK on the Committee for Inaction in Health in 1995. Daily she continues to share her knowledge and wisdom.

Now she is happily married to a kind man called Mr John Lorde my Papa John an intelligent handsome, loving, cricket playing Bajan.

© John Lorde. Mr and Mrs John Lorde. May 2008

*T*he former colony now the Cooperative Republic of Guyana celebrated its 50th birthday a few years ago in 2016 and the PNC government with its 1 seat majority was enjoying electoral success after years in the wilderness of opposition. They decreed that in celebration commemorative arches at a cost of millions of Guyana dollars. Many of the youth were able to see the old films of British Guiana and saw the higher standard of living enjoyed and trains... they rightly asked why it had all been squandered. Many are ready to leave and put all their energy in to study only to migrate when qualified. There is a feeling among them that Guyana needs to reconnect with England and make firmer ties and realise the counties full potential to be a gentle giant in agriculture production and water management. The money for newly found oil should be ploughed into infrastructure to open the country and re build the railway and ports. Education institutions improved and languages of the continent should be taught. Also, every young adult should be able to have training for industry so they can build on the country up. A new fresh leadership needed to be created that will truly be benevolent and honest towards All the people of Guyana. This is the youths hope.

Our personal family story can be replicated thousands of times as each person who boarded the planes and boats to go to colder climes has similar experiences with varying degrees of success and still it continues today ...All the family returned to Christianity and all believe in Jesus as our Lord and Saviour.

So today many people in Guyana now rely on their migrated family members to live by the remittances sent via Western Union and such. It makes the reality of living in 2 places a real dichotomy Home is always something that is sought. My mother says home and from the tone of her voice we know whether she means Guyana or Croydon.

She is extremely happy to be here and grateful for her Guyanese heritage but never forgets where it all started.

Lynette as a student in Taunton. 1959. © Lynette Richards-Lorde.

Douglas Frank

Nancy Richards-Frank as a student nurse.

© Douglas Frank
Mr and Mrs Frank 1962.

FAMILY PICTURES

Ruthy returns to England

Master Adrian Richards aged 3

Sergeant Jonathan in the army at a ceremony in Jerusalem.

Nancy and Lynette in Oxford Mathew Richards with Father Vincent
Richards

Father Goodrich's 90th Birthday
© Lynette Richards-Lorde

Beatrice Richards nee Browne and me at Brighton Beach 1970's©
Lynette Richards-Lorde

80th Birthday Lynette. 2018
© Lynette Richards-Lorde

Mr and Mrs Vincent Richards, Vince and Alicia.

© Vincent Richards

Aunty Pansy Small and Christine-Althea 2018

Lastly, in closing we know we all owe an enormous debt of Gratitude to George Brown, Queenie, John Richards and Beatrice Richards nee Brown who took a firm hold of the baton that was passed and ensured they ran a good race to the finish line where they in turn passed it on to their children and children's children. Mighty men of valour who although materially missed todays luxuries were far ahead of their peers, unselfish in their ways, and thought on a level far ahead of their times. They supported their children ambitions with finance, spirituality, wisdom, unselfishness, advise, genuine good counsel, encouragement and Love.

John Augustus Richards was a man who never travelled far beyond the boundaries of his land of Guyana. Never attended a university but he had attained a 1st class PhD in Common Sense and wealth beyond measure in his family and he is today still highly revered as a gentleman of the highest esteem and reputation renowned for his enlightened thought and cultured style of life always looking to do good deeds and he is today missed by the community he lived in and loved. He lived in the best of times for Guyana and survived the worst, living on through us so we must live up to our namesake as he did to his. John Augustus Richards lived not only for himself but also his lost twin brother, his middle name Augustus meaning venerable, distinguished, accorded a great deal of respect due to his wisdom and character and he is.

John Richards realised that a good name and reputation were essential in life .

We have endeavoured to live up to the name we have inherited.

The Richards name means Powerful and Brave with Levi meaning To be with God.

What more can you need in Life than a good name and reputation?

This true tale can be echoed in almost every street and village where the brightest and the best of the countries of the whole Caribbean left to seek their fortunes overseas... It continues to this day. The dandelion flowers of their families will never be whole again only the memories remain intact.

That we lived cheek by jowl in what may to others seem a simple a small clapboard whitewashed house in a side street but they made our home at

47 Palm Street, Werk-en-Rust, Georgetown take on a value far beyond its monetary value it is for us synonymous with the highest superior meaning of family, security, morality and love. May our ancestors' memories be a blessing always. Amen.

No matter where we may roam or how grand our properties and many material possessions may become, for us family Richards-Brown number 47 Palm Street,

Werk-en-Rust, Georgetown, Guyana, South America will always be our Home.

Jonathan is the great grandson of John Augustus Richards and has by God's grace grown into a lovely young gentleman. He is partner in the family business www.crossroadsmotortours.nl, working with Caricom and Ecowas governments on various infrastructure projects and as property developer worldwide...Here he is with his faithful Sheep dog Monty. We look forward to him settling down with his own family and a blessed beautiful wife and children.

*Jonathan and Monty visit Granny and Grandpa John (c)Lynette
Richards-Lorde.*

Every Blessing.

A few more pictures in closing :

Lynette travelling back to Taunton 2016 for the filming of the BBC film.
"Black Nurses the women who saved the NHS." a Paul Blake Film Production, this time she travelled in the First-Class Carriage of the train .

© Lynette Richards-Lorde

A Handwritten note of Beatrice E Richards relating who her many customers were in Georgetown Guiana from 1934- 1980

Ruthy and her loyal furry friend Mr Rabbit.1966

© Ruthy Richards Levi aka Chrissy .

HE Mrs Gail Teixeria Min of Parliamentary Affairs and Mummy in Guyana High Commission London England, September 2022.

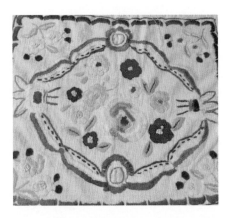

Beatrice Eudora Richards own design and handiwork
© Ruthy.
www.ruthysbooks.com

Lynette was the first black lady to become Unit General Manager Director of Nursing and Midwifery Services, here at St Georges University Hospital,Tooting with her staff.

Mummy with the Mayor of Croydon ...Times change

*Mummy is in the Jack Beula (Nubian Jak) book celebrating Caribbean
and African contribution o the NHS.*

EPILOGUE

*W*e remember Beryl Jodhan, the youngest sister of Beatrice, Pauline,Hilda and Charlie Browne. Daughter of Evangeline "Queen"and George Browne passed away to glory aged 100 in Hamilton Canada surrounded by her family and friends. Pat Jodhan her son, Kevin grandson who she raised both cared for her along with Shannon Kevin's daughter and his wife took care of her in their care home. Beryl was the only one to survive to that great age, still happy, chatty, cheerful and beautiful. May her memory be a blessing always.

Also we recall Father Derek Goodrich who left his good home in Norbury England, to come to preach the Good Word in Guyana. In the process becoming our family and an influencer for good.

*G*uyana has now turned the corner in terms of prosperity and governance it has become a leader in tourism, oil production, education, health care and is becoming a happier safer place full of wonder and beauty. We have a new government with bold ideas and we have thanks to them taken our place in the world stage. Our President HE Dr Irfaan Ali is young, dynamic and educated with excellent connections to UK and especially through new HE High Commissioner, Ms Jane Miller OBE, because of this friendly relationship we the people benefit greatly. We are indeed a blessed land ...British Airways is resuming direct flights to Georgetown after a hiatus of over 50 years to London Gatwick, so many more people will be able to visit loved ones, enjoy eco tourism and do business...and little me Christine will be flying the route too, as in January 2023 my career with BA.com as cabin crew long haul part-time Gatwick starts again...Looking forward to see you on board :) We are truly blessed.

We give thanks for the countless people along the way, characters whose stories deserve their own chapters in books. We hope this our 47 Palm Street Werk-en-Rust gives you an insight into our little family. How they thrived and lived full loving lives regardless the distance or battles and we carry on remembering their pioneering spirit and faith Knowing "I can do all things through Jesus Christ who strengthens me." Amen.

Celebrating Nancy and Freddie's wedding which was happening in Oxford, England at 47 Palm Street Georgetown. We will meet again someday.

*Lynette Richards-Lorde Joint President of Inner Wheel Croydon 2024
www.innerwheel.com Also look at Black Nurses who saved the NHS on
YouTube or the bbc https://youtu.be/9oeibosad7c?si=
oraFawxbhMopiHjM*

Printed in Great Britain
by Amazon

55023503R00112